The People Who Lived Among Us

G.S. Musevich
Translated by Sherwin L. Sokolov

The People Who Lived Among Us
Dedicated to the Suffering of the Jewish People

Original Book in Russian
Copyright © G.S. Musevich, 2009

Translation
Copyright © Sherwin L. Sokolov, 2014
All Right Reserved
ISBN-13: 978-0-692-31755-6
ISBN-10: 0692317554

Translation Dedication

This translation is dedicated to the memory of my brother, Howard H. Sokolov, MD.

About 165 years ago, our great-grandfather, Joseph Sokolowsky, had the foresight to be a pioneer settler of Colony Sarovo to attempt to provide a better life for and ensure the safety of his children and future family generations. Years ago, my brother had the foresight to gather information from our father, Meyer Sokolov, that started my journey into our family's history and ultimately to this book. I will forever be grateful to them.

Sherwin L. Sokolov
2014

Translator's Acknowledgements

I am grateful to the late Mr. Musevich for his written permission to translate his book and to Oleg Medvedevsky for acting as the intermediary with Mr. Musevich and adding to the translation. Further, the kindness of Andrei Ostashenya of www.kamenets.by/ for permission to use the original cover design of Mr. Musevich's book for the cover of the translation is acknowledged. My thanks is also given to a few Russian language speakers, especially Susan Matveyeva, Ph.D., and other individuals that, here and there, contributed information and assistance with the translation, which essentially is the product using multiple reference materials and adjusting the results to reflect Mr. Musevich's meaningfulness and intent. A special note of appreciation is to my wife, Barbara, for her help and encouragement. Mr. Musevich's book in Russian is available online at:
http://kamenets.by/downloads/book/people.pdf

Sherwin L. Sokolov
2014

Table of Contents

	Page
From the Author	1
Preface	2
Activities of the Jews of Kamenets	7
Commerce	
Industry and Crafts	
Agricultural Colonies	
Transportation - A Window Into the World	20
Working Conditions	21
Businesses	
Stores and Shops	
Restaurants and Tea Rooms	
Public Life	23
Education	25
Schools	
Secondary School in Wysokie-Litovsk	
Kamenets-Lithuanian Yeshiva	
Jewish Community ("Kahal") Life	35
Historical Background	
Jewish Community Life in Kamenets-Litovsk	
The Jewish Community Council of Wysokie-Litovsk in 1936	
Kamenets-Litovsk in the Late 19th and Early 20th Century	43
Kamenets-Litovsk in the 20th Years of the 20th Century	44
The Composition of the Population of the Town by Nationality	
Religion, Synagogues, Cemeteries	46
Synagogues	
Cantor Jaffe	
Cemeteries	
Tombstones Found	
Rabbis and Cantors of Kamenets-Litovsk	
Jewish Culture in Kamenets-Litovsk	57
Libraries	
Amateur Theater	
Writers and Poets	
Scientists	

Leisure Time
  Yehezkel Kotik on Kamenets-Litovsk

The Terrible 20th Century — 69
  The Arrival of the Red Army
  War!
  The First Executions of Jews
  The Removal of Jews from Pruzhany and Their Return
  The Ghetto in Kamenets
  The Executions Continued

The Story of Dora Galperin — 81
  Terrible Days and Years
  The Ghetto
  Courage and Escape from the Clutches of Killers and Suffering
  Release
  Out of the Frying Pan and Into the Fire
  In a Soviet Prison
  Court
  Back to Prison
  The End of the Story
  Author's Comments

The Removal of the Jewish Boys for Work — 90

Closing of the Ghetto — 91

In Kamenets Thirty Years Later — 96

Open Letter — 100

The Ashes of the Homes and the People — 102

Summer Flowers For The Doctor — 105

Background — 108
  The Area Population of Jews in 1939
  Occupations of the Residents of Kamenets-Litovsk
  The Number of Jewish and Christian Houses in Kamenets-Litovsk
  Street Names in Kamenets

Epilogue — 116

Sources — 118

Notes — 122

G.S. Musevich
Translated by Sherwin L. Sokolov

The People Who Lived Among Us
Dedicated to the Suffering of the Jewish People

From the Author

In 1500, a Jewish man from Brest named Shleyma Ikhelevich bought a house in Kamenets-Litovsk and this laid the foundation for the settlement of Jews in the town. However, historical sources mention Jews staying in our town in 1465, but it was probably temporary rather than permanent. The Jewish population gradually increased to the beginning of the Second World War and became dominant in Kamenets-Litovsk and in Wysokie-Litovsk. They lived not only in these towns, but also in villages such as Volchin, Ryasno, Verhovichi, and many other villages, and in the agricultural colonies of Lotovo, Sarovo, and Abramovo.

This nation (Jews), with a different religion, different language, different culture, and different customs has not been fully understood by others. And the leaders of a Fascist racial theory incinerated them. But we still stand on the sidelines, not being disturbed by the memory of these terrible events. Those who keep silent about it can involuntarily doom themselves and their descendants in the future to unforeseen misery and misfortune.

I am standing on the threshold of eternity. Therefore, I must not, I do not have the right to carry with me everything that I know, found in documents, and heard from people who were not indifferent and shared their memories. That's why I wrote this book; for living people and their descendants in the future to know what people lived among us. Many of those who shared their memories are no longer alive. To all of them, living and departed, I express my wholehearted and profound thanks: Paul Gorbatzewich, Vladimir Grigorevsky, Leon Gedalia Goldring, Shloma Kantarovich, Vasyl Troychuk, Leo Sachko, Zinaida Krechko, Andrey Kharko, Eugene Keskevich, Jaroslav Mushits, Gregory Zaretsky, Vasyl Demyanchuk, Ryszard Mankovsky, Gariy Kardychkin, Jacob Potoka, Anna Budko, Nicholas Romaniuk, Anna

Musevich, Yuri Saharchuk, Director Anna Terebun, Director of the State Archives of the Brest Region (GABO), the authors of memoirs: Yehezkel Kotik, Dora Galperin, Dov (Berchik) Schmidt, Charles Raddock, Velvel Kustin, Chatskel Kagan, Yitzchak Sheynfeld, Label Golberg, Abram Shudrof, Jan Perdenia, Oleg Medvedevsky, Henry Neugass, Jenni Buch, as well as the translator who translated from English, Irina Borovkova (Makarevich).

Preface

Ancient people – the Jews living in Palestine, after two rebellions and being bloodily and brutally suppressed by the Romans, as described in detail by a contemporary of the time, Josef Matityahu (Titus Flavius Josephus), in "The Jewish War," left their homeland and ended up in the Diaspora. In the first century AD, they went in three main directions – Byzantium, Persia, and the Iberian Peninsula. Deprived of their promised land for many centuries, enduring hardships, privations, and persecution, they were able to return to their ancestral homeland after almost 2,000 years, and were able to establish their sovereign state - Israel.

These people truly suffered. You cannot refute the vast intellectual potential of Jews. They have successfully used it for the good of their people. Among them were many activists with passionate natures. However, their passion was not directed at war, not on conquest, but on peace.

The Jewish religion is ancient. It was there in the first millennium BC and has generated two powerful branches of the world religions - Christianity, which arose in the first half of the first century AD, and Islam, which appeared in the seventh century AD for the first time in the lands of the eastern Slavs, Jews appeared in the time of the Khazar Khanate (Khazaria), where they were merchants and collectors of tribute and taxes. They came to the Kiev provinces, and some reports indicate they even lived in Kiev, where there was a synagogue. From Khazaria they came to Persia and occupied senior positions in diplomacy, administration, and commerce. There they introduced Judaism.

The Jews had to flee from Persia in 529 AD for the following reasons:

A Persian nobleman named Mazdak advanced the theory that existing justice in the world can be corrected by means of reason and the introduction of "equality" of rights and "the equation of wealth," i.e., confiscation of property of the rich. There was a division between the followers of Mazdak and the "supporters of evil," i.e., those who did not agree with Mazdak. How history repeats itself a lot, changing in shape and staying essentially the same! All this was repeated in Russia after the revolution 1917. Much of the Jewish community in Persia supported Mazdak. However, Prince Hozroy (Khosrau) was offended by Mazdak and his supporters. He gathered a large army of men and ruthlessly destroyed them and hung Mazdak, and, as mentioned above, the Jews, supporters of Mazdak, had to run away from Persia. They settled in the North Caucasus in the valley between the Terek and Sulak rivers in the Byzantine Empire, the land of the Eastern Slavs, and later in Western Europe.

Circumstances were such that the Jews began to develop international trade, creating a pivotal trading point stretching from the Pyrenees Mountains to China that was protected by diplomatic action and foreign military forces. The Jews, as history shows in different countries and different states, are symbiotic with the powers that be that needed money and had the ability to conduct free trade and engage in money lending and crafts. In this way, their well-being depended on the location and the favor or disfavor at the helm of power. So it was in Persia, the Khazar Kaganate, Spain, France, Germany, and other countries. When the Jews lost the favor of the authorities in some states and were harassed, they migrated to another state. Religion played a role in this.

Tracing the history of the Jewish people in Europe, there is movement from the East to Spain, Portugal, France, Germany, and the Netherlands. Seven centuries ago, they moved first to Poland, and then to the Grand Duchy of Lithuania of Vytautas the Great in times when the borders were wide open to Jews. Here they found a favorable life. During the 15th and 16th centuries, they were widely settled throughout the Lithuanian Duchy that included Ukraine and Belarus, but mainly in cities and towns. They were granted the right engage in trade, money lending, renting and leasing property, and crafts.

The Jews not only moved West in our land, they also went East much earlier than to the West. We have less information about this, but there is some information. In the Galicia-Volyn Chronicle, the chronicler, describing the death of Prince of Volyn Vladimir (John) Vasilkovich in 1289 and the grief of representatives of different nationalities, refers to Jews: "All of the residents of Vladimir cried over him (Prince Vladimir) [when he died], men, women, children, foreigners, former residents of Surozh, people from Novgorod, and Jews, who wept as at the time of the capture of Jerusalem, when they all were in captivity in Babylon..." [Life of the Prince of Volyn Vladimir (John) Vasilkovich]. This means that Jews lived in Vladimir-Volyn in the 13th century! Hence, we can assume that the town, founded by Prince Vladimir (John) Vasilkovich, had Jewish merchants.

The Jews enjoyed great privileges. For example, Stefan Batory, on becoming King of Poland, confirmed the previous privileges of the Jewish communities (kahals). Jews were provided with the same rights as the Christian town dwellers (burghers). It was at this time that an increased number of Jews were engaged in crafts.

The organizers of anti-Semitic pogroms were severely punished in the spirit and letter of the Casimir's Privileges. Thus, Stefan Batory strove to ensure conditions of peaceful coexistence of the local population and the Jews, having need for their functions as managers, money lenders, and tenants, and having exclusive rights as buyers of agricultural products.

During the 16th and 17th centuries and later, Jews were major tavern operators, collectors of customs duty, and farmers. A local branch of the Brest Customs House was established in Kamenets-Litovsk.

In 1518, Sigismund I the Old, King of Poland, gave Abram Yezofovich an eight-year lease to collect "customs in Beresteye (Brest) along with all old customs as was established by King Casimir, including the Kamenets branch to take customs duties on roads and ferries as it was from the old time of our father." The Kamenets local branch was located between Zamosty and Kamenets-Litovsk. If you go from Zamosty, the branch was on the right next to the river before the bridge.

In 1529, King Sigismund gave Isaac Yezofovich a three-year lease (exclusive right to collect taxes) for the Kamenets local branch of the Customs House for an annual payment of 2600 kopecks and 333 Hungarian zlotys, with a reduction in future payments for three more years.

In 1569, Kamenets-Litovsk gave a total annual payment of 230 kopecks (pence) to the Royal Treasury in Grodno for its monopoly on vodka.

Jews settled in towns, shtetls, and villages in the Kamenets area. Closer to our times (in the second half of the eighteenth century) they founded three agricultural colonies.

Along with the resettlement of Jews was active transformation of the Jewish community settlements (kahals). Following the settlement of Jews in the Kamenets kahal, there were ups and downs and good and evil. Along with the general population of the land, they suffered and were killed in wars (Polish-Moscovite War, "Swedish Deluge," the Great Northern War, First World War, Polish-Soviet War), and died from epidemics and fires. The tragic consequences of World War II will be discussed separately.

Over the centuries, an opinion was formed that the Jews lived an isolated life in a closed world, observing with neutrality the events going on around them. But this is far from being true. Sometimes, some of them struggled to get out of that world and actively participated in events. For example, take the Tadeusz Kosciuszko Uprising. The Jewish regiment commanded by Colonel Berek Joselewicz participated in the fighting on the side of the Warsaw rebels. Incidentally, in the early twenties of the 20th century, Litewska Street (now Pivnenko Street) was named after Berek Joselewicz, but then, as result of a change of policy of the Polish government, the name was changed.

Sometimes there was friction between Jews and the local population, but open hostility was not observed. Solid, orderly community (kahal) life with well-established rules and laws contributed to greater mutual prosperity and kept out difficult and serious situations. Specific isolation of the social, cultural, and religious life of Jews did not give others a chance to get acquainted with the life of the Jewish population. The local population (I'm not talking about visiting people) watched Jewish life as a joke through a keyhole. Unfortunately, we did not get in touch with Jewish life in Kamenets and comprehend it. We gathered crumbs from scarce, written sources, which perhaps were not always reliable. Here are some observations and generalizations about Jewish life in Kamenets-Litovsk until the establishment of Soviet power.

Jews treated the education of their children with great care, preferring their own education to public education to develop their culture. The focus of attention was always on the maintenance of the synagogue.

Before World War II, the sources of income for the Jewish population were mainly trades, money lending, and crafts. Among the Jews were blacksmiths, tanners, carpenters, shoemakers, tailors, and others. A small number of Jews engaged in agriculture, the transport of cargo and passengers, the collection of secondary raw materials, operating bakeries, and other kinds of work. Almost all local industries were in the hands of the Jews.

From the depths of the Kahal emerged political parties - General Jewish Labor Union of Lithuania, Poland, and Russia–Socialist (BUND), Zionist Party, "Poalei Zion," etc. Some Jews joined the Communist Party of Western Belarus and the Communist Union of Youth, commonly known as Komsomol. Stratification (i.e., social division) of the Jews began.

The establishment of Soviet power in 1939 dramatically changed the life of Jewish communities, and significantly disrupted their social standards that were established for centuries.

Fewer and fewer Jewish names are stored in the memory of the citizens of Kamenets. And, if some of the names managed to have been kept in mind, the majority, I am afraid, are gone forever along with their owners.

The second part of the Second World War began in June 1941 and brought tragic events to the people of Kamenets land. The Germans came. Then followed the first shootings, the first victims. The invaders labeled all Jews with yellow stars. The Nazis forced them to hang the same star on their homes. The Jews were all moved to a ghetto. Only a few Jews survived the Holocaust, this terrible tragedy. The Jews of Kamenets who immigrated to other countries before the war, particularly to the United States, remained alive and escaped the hell of war. Remind the descendants of Kamenets Jews who occasionally visit Kamenets and Wysokie to see the land where their relatives were born, grew up, loved, bore children, worked, died, and were buried.

Unfortunately, most of the homes of Jews did not survive for different reasons. Most of the synagogues were destroyed or the buildings were changed beyond recognition. The Jewish cemetery was wiped out. What do we have as remembrances? Actually nothing!

In the distance abroad are museum pieces from the life of Kamenets Jews. The Kamenetzer Yeshiva survived in the United States and in Israel. There are Jewish Kamenets-Litovsk and Wysokie-Litovsk associations in some countries. This book is a tribute to the people who lived in Kamenets and were incinerated in the Holocaust. This is an attempt to gather the crumbs from the stories of people who lived among us, and to bring the sorrowful truth to the reader.

Activities of the Jews of Kamenets

Commerce

There is a view that all Jews were merchants. Of course, they were engaged in businesses, but not all, as shown in the Table of Occupations (shown later in the book). It can be seen that the Jews worked in 46 occupations; however, many of them did engage in commerce.

In Kamenets-Litovsk before World War II, there were 186 merchants and shopkeepers, and every merchant and shopkeeper had assistants from among relatives and employees. The number of Jews in Kamenets-Litovsk engaged in commerce exceeded 50% of the Jewish population. Selling, finance, and commercial transactions were conducted through the Credit Bank of Kamenets-Litovsk. Christians, who lived on Senatorska Street (now

Pervomayskaya Street) and Litewska Street (now Pivnenko Street), were engaged in agriculture.

Jewish commerce had its own specific methods and techniques that were developed over hundreds of years. First is a narrow specialization in the sale of goods. Second, hard competition. In this case, the winner regarding quality and price is the buyer. Third, a Jewish merchant, in the absence of getting money from the buyer, could sell goods on credit. Fourth, mediation. For example, a Jewish middleman would buy from a chicken farmer and sell the chickens to a wealthier Jew. At the outskirts of Kamenets-Litovsk, Jewish middlemen intercepted peasants traveling to the fair and bought and then sold the goods in Kamenets-Litovsk. Jewish merchants did not wait for buyers to enter their shops to buy something. They loudly invited buyers into their shops, pulling them vigorously by their sleeves into the shops, leaving no chance for them to leave without buying. Customers that constantly bought goods in a shop run by a Jewish merchant were treated specially.

The Jews did not shy away from providing services. Customers who constantly bought goods in a shop run by a Jew were specially treated. For instance, Mankovsky, a landowner coming from Khodosy Dolny to church in Kamenets on a Sunday or a festival would stop on his way to of Moshe Wapniarski on Bialostocka Street (now Pogranichnaya Street) to give him instructions about what he wanted to buy. Returning home, Mankovsky picked up his purchases and from this Wapniarski made a profit.

The Jews not only sold, but also bought agricultural products for themselves from the peasants.

Business was conducted every day in Kamenets-Litovsk, except on the Sabbath (Shabbat) and Jewish holidays when it stopped.

Business was also conducted on adjacent streets. On Market Square, there were two rows of unheated wooden stalls, popularly called "budami" by the people. On hot summer days, the stalls created a pleasant shade. In the cold of winter, women basically traded. They wore hoods, long scarves, and knee-high boots, and put out a pan with hot coals to keep warm. Shops were the main source of a living for many. They were dismantled in 1940 due to the fact that the Soviet government did not recognize private commerce.

The streets adjacent to the area around the Tower, where the gymnasium (i.e., high school) and its athletic field are now, were completely built up with Jewish houses. This development also took place in Wysokie-Litovsk and Volchin. Only there, the rows of stalls were made of brick.

Fairs and markets were the main source of income. They were held every Thursday and also on the 5th and 18th of each month. In addition, there were eight annual fairs:

1. A week before Lent.
2. Evdokievskaya Fair on March 14th.
3. Saint Week Fair (before Orthodox Easter – date varies from the 2nd half of April to the 1st or 2nd week of May).
4. Saint George (Georgievskaya) Feast Day Fair – May 6th on the Gregorian calendar (corresponds to April 23rd on the Julian calendar).
5. Onufrievskaya Fair on June 25th.
6. Saint Simeon (Simeonovskaya) Feast Day Fair on September 14th.
7. Mikhaylovsky (Mikhaylovskaya) Fair on November 21st.
8. Saint Barbara (Varvarinskaya) Feast Day Fair on December 17th.

The most famous fair was the Mikhailovsky Fair, which attracted a huge number of people from near and distant villages.

Markets were held at Church Square, where now there also is a market. The fairs were held at Church Square, on Targovitse Street between today's home of the Zhukovs and the sawmill of the Service Center ("Bytkombinat") on Kobrynska Street (now Chkalova Street), at Market Square (now Lenina Street), and on the following streets: Bialostocka (now Pogranichnaya Street), Bialowiezska, Ogrodova, Doyazd (now Pogranichnaya Street and Naberezhnaya Street), Senatorska (1st of May Street), Przesmyk (Lenina Street), Polna (now Gogolya Street), Dolina (now Proletarskaya Street), Brzeska (now Brestskaya Street), and part of Litewska Street (now Pivnenko Street).

The people from nearby villages came to Kamenets-Litovsk to make purchases and to sell their products. They brought cows, calves, lambs, horses, chickens, ducks, geese, eggs, grains, fruits, vegetables, hides, and wood to be sold. The sale of animals was at Targovitsa (near the present timber sawmill of Service Center). The rest of the products were traded at the Church Square (now the bazaar). Resellers met those traveling to the fair in the outskirts of Kamenets-Litovsk, trying to buy products and to then resell them at a higher price in the town. Artisans from Pruzhany, Shereshevo, and other places brought barrels, buckets, wooden tubs/bathtubs, churns (for churning butter), and other wood products. Potters brought pots, bowls, and pitchers.

At the entrance to Kamenets-Litovsk, tax collectors collected sales tax from those travelling to the fair to sell goods. The collectors were young Jewish boys. The peasants repeatedly expressed dissatisfaction with the fees.

At the time of the fairs, traders hired young men and women to look after the goods to be sold that were specially brought from Brest and other cities. They were paid 1.5 zlotys per day.

Shopkeepers exhibited colored scarves and shiny shoes right at the entrance. They sold inexpensive clothes, which buyers immediately tried on. Wainwrights suggested wheels. Blacksmiths shod horses. The mills ground grain, flax, and vegetable oil squeezed out of rapeseeds. The merchants of iron products offered nails, scythes, axes, pitchforks, shovels/spades, harrows, plows, and other equipment needed by the villagers. Bakers worked diligently to supply stalls with fresh bread, rolls, and packages of bagels and crackers. Gaynovsky from Hajnowka brought an excellent kvass (brew). Shopkeeper Bale Hosh sold soda water from a copper container that was wrapped in cloth. Boyko sold chocolate ice cream, and Linder and Moniz sold ice on Brzeska Street. Different types of halva, candies, sweets, and delicacies aroused the appetites of the buyers.

At the marketplace, the peasants went into tea and snack bars, ate bread and herring, drank vodka, ate fried fish and cucumbers, and cursed. Loud cries from shopkeepers enticed buyers that if they were not going to buy products, then at least look at them.

The crowd went back and forth randomly, buying, selling, or just stopping and staring. There were endless disputes about prices. Shouts and the clapping of hands were heard. This meant that someone had entered into a transaction. Those residents of Kamenets-Litovsk that did not buy or sell anything just stuck with the crowd, watching the events that were happening.

An organ-grinder also playing a drum had a parrot and sold horoscopes. Peasant women were willing to pay a few pennies to learn their fate.

Among the people at the fair was a blind man with a guide. A lot of people gathered around him in the churchyard. He was Ivan Vlasyuk, a lyre player from Volyn, who performed religious songs to the accompaniment of the lyre.

A visit to the fair was not complete without visiting pickpockets. The shouts of their victims filled the air with loud cries that continued for a long time.

At sunset, the fairs ended and all of the shopkeepers left with their products in horse-drawn carts.

Industry and Crafts

At different times, the Jews living in the settlements had manufacturing facilities, which they owned or leased. In the 19th century, in the village of Volchin, the Melbauer wool factory operated. In Kamenets-Litovsk, there was the Brzestowski factory that was rented to David Afraimovich and Hirsch Yudelevich and produced paper and cardboard products. In 1801, the factory produced 1680 reams of paper in the amount of 1810 rubles that year.

In Wysokie-Litovsk, the Leyba Vargaftik, a merchant of the second guild (craft association) opened a wool factory. For various technological operations, there were 22 machines, two presses, four dye boilers, and 12 looms. There was a fulling mill machine operated by a water mill, a machine for carding wool, and a "Wolf" (for crushing fleece before carding) that was horse-driven.

In 1828, the factory produced 11,600 meters of 1st, 2nd, 3rd, and 4th grades of cloth. The workers at the factory were 1 manager, 14 masters, 12 journeymen and apprentices, and 50 laborers, totaling 77 people, including 72 Jews.

Before World War II, Jews in Kamenets-Litovsk owned a number of businesses. On Brzeska Street, Yoselya Shostakovsky had a power plant. On Kobrynskoy Street (now Chkalov Street), Rubin Movsha owned a windmill turbine. There was a steam mill in Peski and another in Zamosty and 4 windmills and a brewery in Staryshov. There were 3 blacksmith shops, a manufacturer of ceramic tiles, and a brickyard owned by Chiam Polyakevich on Brzeska Street, a distillery in Kamenets-Litovsk on Litewska Street (now Pivnenko Street), 8 bakeries, 2 wool combing and carding shops, a lemonade factory on Smocza Street, and a leather tanning business ("garbarnya") on Dojazd Street. These were the main businesses in the town.

The number of Jews engaged in trades reached 300 people, including 12 butchers, 13 tailors, and 48 shoemakers.

Agricultural Colonies

There are two myths. According to one, Jews cannot and do not want to farm. According to the other, Jews did not qualify as soldiers. There are many stories and anecdotes on these subjects, but they are not factual. In the last world war (WWII), several hundred thousand Jews fought in the armies of different countries against Hitler's coalition. Jews fought in the Soviet Army and were enlisted men and officers. Among the officers were generals. They were also heroes of the Soviet Union. In the independent state of Israel, there is compulsory military service for men and women. They have proven that they know how to fight very well.

As a rule, Jews did not engage in agriculture, because they did not own land due to the laws of many countries prohibiting them from owning land. However, Jews found the opportunity to engage in agriculture.

In the past, in the vicinity of Kamenets-Litovsk and Wysokie-Litovsk, there were dozens of estates. The administrators and tenant operators were mainly Jews. Each landowner had two Jews on his estate, an advisor and a director of business affairs. These posts were hereditary, passing from father to son.

Some Jews lived in nearby settlements and engaged in farming. There also were agricultural colonies in the Kamenets area. Most of the population of the Kamenets region in the past, as well as now, lived in rural areas and had to physically work hard on the land. Over hundreds of years, a psychology of the rural worker developed. The villagers believed, and still believe, that those who do not work on the land are loafers. This is partly preserved in the psychology of urban residents – natives and immigrants from villages. Because of this psychology, a friction arose between the Jews and rest of the population. The condition of aversion or rejection of Jews by certain parts of the population is called "anti-Semitism." In the past, not like present times, anti-Semitism was not shown toward all Jews. It was shown toward specific individuals. The tensions sometimes developed into pogroms against the Jews. Pogroms did not occur in the Kamenets area.

Generally, the image of the enemy in one form or another has existed throughout the history of mankind. The image of the enemy is a convenient screen behind which woes, troubles, disorders, failures, and displeasure with everyday life and at the national level can be hidden. But when anti-Semitism develops into a government policy, as happened in Nazi Germany and its occupied territories, the mass extermination of civilians was inevitable. Fascists in occupied territories subjected Jews to the Holocaust (burning, incineration, and physical destruction). The same happened in the Kamenets District. Not more than 40 people survived. They are the ones who went abroad before the war. Only three of them that endured the Holocaust survived.

But back to the topic of agriculture and childhood memories of colonist Velvel Kustin and Sarovo Christian resident Gregory Zaretsky. At the beginning of the eighteenth century, more than 500 Jewish families lived in Kamenets area villages. Some rented taverns, others, as mentioned above, served on the estates of landlords. In the early years of the eighteenth century, there were 58 taverns. By 1784, the number had grown to 86. Later it was significantly reduced when the Jews who rented the taverns in the villages returned to Kamenets-Litovsk and Wysokie-Litovsk. Although rare, there were cases of Jewish employment in agriculture. It was also so in the Kamenets region. The story will now continue about Jewish agricultural colonies.

There were three Jewish agricultural colonies – Lotovo, Sarovo, and Abramovo. They were located northwest of Kamenets-Litovsk. Lotovo was on the right side of the Kamenets-Abelian Road, Sarovo was 0.5 km from the Kamenets-Kamenyuki Road, and Abramovo was on the left side of Kamenets-Kamenyuki Road, between the villages of Makovishche and Kamenyuki.

These colonies were formed around the beginning of the eighteenth century.[1] The first colony established was Lotovo, then Sarovo, and then Abramovo. It should be noted that Abramovo is mentioned in "Old Certificates" in 1700. The colonies were named in honor of the biblical characters, Lot, Sarah, and Abraham, the progenitor/patriarch of the Jewish people.

Although the original reasons for the formation of the colonies is unknown, there is a legend that claims that settlement in rural districts and employment in agriculture was one of the ways to avoid military service that lasted many years. By law, landowners were exempt from military service.

Life on the colonies can be seen in the colony of Sarovo. Originally the colony consisted of 24 families, each of which received 25 hectares of land from the Russian authorities after the partition of Poland. The first colonists were natives of Brest-Litovsk where they engaged in commerce and merchant activities. For example, Herschel Lichtser Kustin produced and sold candles. The names of some of the other settlers were Eliezer Ashkenazi, Joseph Sokolowsky, Herschel Zaydinger, Moshe Zimovich, Kravetsky, and Chorny.

Year after year, the colonists worked the land, sowing, plowing, and harvesting. They kept cows, horses, and poultry. They were released from paying taxes. Children grew up and families expanded. Income from their labor became inadequate. The children, not having the possibility to buy land, went to the city of Brest-Litovsk, from which the first settlers came, and to

Kamenets-Litovsk, and began to work as drivers/coachmen and millers. The colonists that remained, and were able to, bought the land. Those without the money to buy land leased or rented it.

Among the second generation of colonists was Israel Ashkenazi, who did not want to return to Brest-Litovsk. Instead, he went to Palestine and became one of the founders of the colony "Yesud HaMa'ala" in Upper Galilee. Israel Ashkenazi taught the new European settlers to Palestine how to plow and sow. He brought his father and mother, Eliezer and Gitel Ashkenazi, to Palestine. Their descendants are numerous and they settled in different parts of the country. They still live in Yesud HaMa'ala and in other parts of Israel. One of the descendants of Eliezer Ashkenazi died in defense of Kfar Giladi in 1946. Their whole story is told in two books written in Hebrew.

The Kustin family was the only one whose descendants remained in the colonies for the lifetime of four generations. The ancestor of the family, Herschel Lichtser Kustin, had an only son, Velvel. Herschel bought 25 hectares of available land and another 25 from colonists who had gone back to town. Because of the large amount of land, he was able to secure his family's income from farming.

Velvel had four sons and three daughters. The daughters married and lived in surrounding villages. One of the sons was Moishe Yosel. The sons leased the land of colonists that had left the colony. The leased land supplemented their own land, but this did not improve living conditions much and Velvel's sons began to leave, one after the other, to distant America.

Returning home in 1909 from his second trip to America (he traveled to America to earn money), Velvel's son, Moishe Yosel, bought another 15 hectares, doubling his property. He also bought 10 head of cattle, some horses, and began to raise chickens and ducks. In a short time, he became a well-established colonist (in Soviet times called a "*Kulak*").

The main element of the life of the colonists was their spiritual life. There was religion and education of the children. Therefore, the first colonists not only built houses and farm buildings, they erected a Beit Midrash (religious house), which combined a synagogue and a religious school. It had a simple architectural form and looked unpretentious. The roof was covered with straw. Outside there was a plaque, indicating that it was the Beit Midrash. Inside was the Ark of the Covenant supported by two lions, one on each side. Two Torahs were kept inside the Ark, and above it stood the Tablets of the Covenant. In the center of room, surrounded by six columns, was the "bimah." The ceiling was decorated with stars and the signs of the zodiac on a dark blue field.

Prayers in the Beit Midrash were read three times a day, with different colonists alternating. After the service, many remained to study the Talmud.

Religious education of the children was conducted in one of the rooms of the Beit Midrash. Studies began at 7:00 in the morning and ended at 8:00 in the evening. The school's teachers were Rabbis Eliezer Rogoznitsky, Pinya Rappoport, and Yosel Turk, and a dayan (religious judge), Rabbi Lazer Velvel of Zamosty. The latter came to pray at the Beit Midrash before holidays. During his visits, he asked for contributions for poor Jews. By the time of his departure, a committee of the colonists collected a wagon loaded with donations of wheat, rye, and potatoes.

The colonists observed the Sabbath (Saturday) very strictly. By virtue of the strict prohibition of all work on this day, orthodox (devout) Jews did not work. Therefore, on Sabbath and holidays, work was carried out by payment to peasants from neighboring villages. They fed the livestock and poultry, milked the cows, and stoked the furnaces in the winter.

Relations with Christians were peaceful, and sometimes even friendly. Ivan the Shepherd (it was a nickname) occupied a special place. His job was to herd the colonists' cows. Additionally, he was a Sabbath-goy (a non-Jew, carrying on work on Saturday). Ivan put out the lamps in the Beit Midrash and stoked the furnace in the winter. He was devoted to the colonists. After World War I, when the colony lacked ritual objects ["Esrogim" ("Lemons" - citrons) and "Luluvs" (Palm Branches)] for the celebration of Sukkot, the Feast of Tabernacles, Ivan ran 4 kilometers to Zamosty, where the ceremonial items were available, took them with him, and ran to Sarovo, After the service, he ran back, carrying the ritual objects.

The children of the colonists had the right to attend school in Belyovo, where the Russian language was taught and, when it was Poland, the Polish language was taught. But the children did not attend school there. The parents, despite financial difficulties, maintained and supported continuous and regular education in the colony's Beit Midrash. They did not forget about the Bible passage that is repeated in the Prayer Book, "... and you should teach your children diligently."

When it was necessary to hire a teacher, it was never an inexpensive one. The teacher was to be one of the best, not only a good teacher, but also a versatile expert with secular knowledge. For this the colonists had to pay good money, and many parents had difficulty with this. They borrowed money from wheat dealers in Kamenets-Litovsk, with the next year's crop as security. The teacher was not only well paid, but he was also provided with food and housing.

The colonists did not pay taxes to the Religious Community Council (Kahal). Everything associated with religious life was carried out by the elected Community Council. The elections were held on the night of Simchat Torah, when the "Gabai" (chief officer) was also elected. That honor in the colony was given to Moishe Yosel Kustin each year, and he served in that capacity all of his life. On the night of Simchat Torah, it was usual for the Gabai to address the general meeting about the costs of community needs, and the homeowners promised to pay them in installments.

There was no cemetery in the colony. The dead were buried in Kamenets-Litovsk. But there were other expenses. On major holidays, a paid cantor (religious singer and reciter of prayers) was brought from Kamenets-Litovsk. He was called Shlomo Lisker, because he came from the village of Liski where he worked for a wealthy landowner who was not Jewish. He was the manager of the farm. He also had to watch that cattle did not wander from the estate's fields at night and spoil crops. Because of the cattle spoiling crops, some farm owners threatened to kill him and he left the village. His nickname followed him and survived, and was transformed into the name Lisker.

An important aspect of religious life was the repair of the Beit Midrash (religious house). After Moshe Yosel Kustin returned from his second trip to America in 1909, the colony decided that the Beit Midrash was in need of repair. Each member of the colony gave a financial contribution and also participated in the renovation and repair of the building. The most active in the renovation project were Velvel Kustin, Moshe Yosel Kustin, his sons Ruven, Labe, Herschel, and his brother Ephraim Simon.

The life of the colonists in Lotovo and Abramovo was nearly the same. The colonists were engaged in agriculture. Individual Jews, such as Elya Glombovski of Kamenets-Litovsk, had 20 hectares of land that he cultivated and on which he kept five cows and two horses. Mendel of Zamosty (a suburb of Kamenets-Litovsk) had 20 hectares of cultivated land.

The colonies existed until 1941. Now there is none. In the interwar period (1920-1939), life on the Sarovo colony can be traced using the recollections of Gregory Zaretsky. Eight Jewish families lived in Sarovo with Ukrainians, who came from Shcherbovo, Novitskovichi, Krivlyany, and other villages. The Jews had 16 to 20 hectares of land, 2 to 3 cows, and a horse. Pigs were not kept because their religious beliefs did not allow it. All lived amicably. The children played together and one woman said that her sister was fluent in Yiddish. The local residents were treated by the Jews, including healing Gregory Zaretsky's father.

The colonists had their own butcher, a man who had the right to slaughter cattle as permitted by religious law. Such meat was called "kosher." If the slaughter was committed by a "goy" (a non-Jew), the meat was considered "treyf" (i.e., not Kosher) and Jews were not allowed to eat it.

When the Nazis came, the Jews in Kamenets-Litovsk were taken to a ghetto from which they never returned. The Nazis did to them what they did to all Jews. There is only a memory of the names of the heads of households:

Chiam Chorny, Yosel Soroko, brothers David and Shimshel Zaydinger, and brothers Leiba, Bobel, and Froim and Yankel Kustin.

The former colony no longer exists. There is no synagogue that stood in the center of the village on the road to Belyovo. The homes of the colonists do not exist. The village of Sarovo has gone into oblivion. There are only eight houses in which Christians live. They are elderly and are at the threshold of eternity.

Abramovo was the biggest Jewish colony. After the return of the refugees to the reborn Poland, many Jews began to sell their land and farms, and leave for towns and cities where the Polish authorities gave them preferential treatment in commerce and craft occupations. In their place, came Ukrainian peasants. In 1939, before the war, Abramovo had only 20 Jewish and 12 Christian households. Here again Christians and Jews lived together in peace.

In 1941, when the Nazis came, the first thing they did was to take all of the colonists to the Bialystok ghetto where they shared the fate of all of the Kamenets area Jews. In the same year, the Germans began the destruction of all settlements in the Bialowieza Forest. The residents were taken out and the villages were burned together with the Christian church in Belaya. The invaders suggested that the Christian residents of Abramovo disassemble their homes and transport them to a neighboring village, Makovishche. The Jewish homes were burned. After the war, Abramovo peasants moved back to their homes in Abramovo. Abramovo was revived, but without Jews. In Abramovo, there are 4 houses and 7 residents.

The years have passed. There are no Jewish agricultural colonies in the Kamenets area. Lotovo disappeared from the face of the earth and the villages of Sarovo and Abramovo are ready to sink into oblivion.

When someone or something leaves us forever, feelings of grief encompass us. It is not in our power to change it. It is God's will!

Transportation – A Window Into the World

When the Moscow to Warsaw railway was built, there was supposed to be a branch from Zhabinka to Bialystok and the border with East Prussia, but the project was rejected, because the pristine silence of a dense forest, the Bialowieza Forest, would be broken. Instead of Kamenets-Litovsk, the branch passed through Wysokie-Litovsk (tens of kilometers from Kamenets-Litovsk) away from the Bialowieza Forest and the planned direction. Only cartage remained in the town until a bus later appeared in Kamenets-Litovsk.

Cartage for freight and passengers was by cabs (horse-drawn carts). There were 20 cabs drivers or, as they were referred to in Kamenets-Litovsk, "balagol." The cab drivers were paid reasonably well. This was the main mode of transport for passengers and transporting goods

In the 30th year of the twentieth century, a lorry (truck) came to Kamenets-Litovsk. The owners of the vehicle were Osher Stempnitsky and Moishe Resnick.

There was a bus from Brest-Litovsk to Kamenets-Litovsk. The first stop was on Market Square. Later, a bus station was built on Brzeska Street. Travel to Brest-Litovsk cost 1 zloty.

Traffic increased, especially after a new route opened from Brest-Litovsk to Zhabinka to Kamenets-Litovsk. For Jewish youth, it opened a window to the world. The bus made it possible to go to Brest-Litovsk. They also went in search of a better life in the United States, Argentina, Cuba, Palestine, and Australia.

The bus station was on Brzeska Street and it attracted young and old people. They came there to meet an arriving bus, to hear the news, get greetings from Brest-Litovsk or Zhabinka, and to look at the "new faces" of people coming to Kamenets-Litovsk from other cities. Theatrical companies began to come to Kamenets-Litovsk by bus more often.

Working Conditions

In Kamenets-Litovsk there were great merchants, shoemakers, tailors, furriers, carpenters, blacksmiths, tanners, wainwrights, and other experts in their fields. But only one or two out of three craftsmen built their own house. The youth had difficulty learning crafts, trades, and acquiring professions. Incomes for skilled workers were insufficient and it was difficult at times to make ends meet. There was a trade union of tailors in the town. They went on strike once. As a result, tailors and seamstresses had an 8-hour work day and better working conditions. A strike was also declared by shoemakers, but it did not achieve a reduction in working hours.

Businesses

Before World War II, the following businesses were in Kamenets-Litovsk:

1. Making collars - 1
2. Making carts - 4
3. Vegetable oil (Oleyarni) shops – 3
4. Mill - 4
5. Brewery (Brewing) - 1
6. Distillery Plant -1
7. Windmill - 4
8. Forge -3
9. Power plant – 2
10. Bakery - 8
11. Watchmaker -2
12. Wool carder – 2
13. Bootmaker shop -1
14. Shingles manufacturing shop -1
15. Concrete plant - 2
16. Tinsmith shop - 1
17. Tile plant - 1
18. Brickyard - 1
19. Carpentry shop - 3
20. Hairdresser - 2

21. Leather tanning ("garbarnya") - 1
23. Repair shop -3
24. Soap making shop – 3
25. Candle manufacturing - 2
26. Feather processing shop - 1
27. Socks maker shop - 1
28. Carpentry workshop - 3
29. Lemonade factory - 1
30. Shoemaker shop – 6
31. Harness maker shop - 1
32. Bicycle repair - 1
33. Locksmith - 2
34. The company operating the forest - 1
35. Sheep skins tanning shop - 1
36. Hotel - 1
Total: 86

Stores and Shops

1. Candle shop - 3
2. Lumber store - 1
3. Frames and glass shop -2
4. Brick and tile store - 2
5. Bicycle shop - 1
6. Ice cream shop - 2
7. Butcher shop - 1
8. Grain store - 1
9. Book store – 1
10. Fishing tackle and bait shop - 1
11. Fabric shop - 3
12. Hardware and ironware store - 9
13. Ready-to-wear clothing shop - 5
14. Wine store - 2
15. Tobacco products shop - 4
16. Leather products shop – 4
17. Grocery (Food) store – 48

18. Salt and spice shop - 1
19. Horse sales – 1
20. Haberdashery/dry goods shop - 13
21. Yeast shop - 1
22. Kitchen equipment shop - 1
23. Seed, fertilizer, chemicals shop - 1
24. Stationery shop - 1
25. Feather shop - 2
26. Pharmacy - 2
Total: 113 shops + 73 stores = 186

Restaurants and Tea Rooms

The inhabitants of Kamenets-Litovsk, visitors, and participants in the fairs had restaurants and tea rooms at their disposal. There were 2 restaurants and 13 tea rooms. Service was offered at all times to the rich and the poor and the meals appealed to all tastes.

Public Life

Jews played a role in the life of Kamenets area community organizations, such as the Society for the Guardianship of the Elders ("Pitz-Chiam"); "Tog-Chiam," a Society for the Care/Guardianship of Orphans; "TOZ," an "Emigration Society"; "Zhaz," the union of shoemakers; an orphanage; a home for the elderly; a philanthropic society, "Linat Tzedek"; and a Cultural/Educational Society, "Tarbut."

There were grassroots structures of various political parties, such as Zionist, Jewish Peoples Party, Jewish Workers' Party (Communist), Jewish Individual Party, "Poalei Zion" (Lyevitsa), BUND (General Jewish Labor Union of Lithuania, Poland, and Russia–Socialist) "Gordoniya," and "Beitar," whose members also included a volunteer fire brigade and a brass band of 54 people under the leadership of Zajac. A youth group, "Freedom," organized meetings that promoted the idea of a Jewish society based on socialist principles. Some Jews were in cells of the Communist Party of Western Belarus and the Communist Union of Youth.

The parties were active and involved in the elections of the Polish government and created conditions for favorable decisions.

Indicative in this respect were the municipal elections to the commune/municipal councils of Wysokie-Litovsk and Kamenets-Litovsk in the year 1927.

In Wysokie-Litovsk, there were 1,267 people eligible to vote. 1,010, or 80%, voted. Voting took place by voters having to select 12 municipal council members (radni) from 8 parties.

The results were as follows:

List number 1 - Zionists - 2 seats
List number 2 - Jewish Individual Party - 1 seat
List number 3 - The Christian Individual Party – 0 seats
List number 4 - Communists - 2 seats
List number 5 - The Jewish Popular Party - 0 seats
List number 6 - The Jewish Party - 0 seats
List number 7 - The Jewish Peoples Party - 4 seats
List number 8 – BUND (Jewish Socialist Labor Party) - 3 seats
Total: 12 seats, 12 Municipal council members (radni)

In Kamenets-Litovsk there were 1,205 people eligible to vote. 1,054, or 87.5%, voted. There were six parties from which to choose 12 municipal council members (radni).

The results were as follows:

List number 1 - Individual Christian Party – 1 seat
List number 2 - PPS (Polska Partia Sotsialistychna – Polish Socialist Party) – 0 seats
List number 3 - Jewish Labor Party (Communist) - 2 seats
List number 4 - Civilian Non-Partisan Party - 5 seats
List number 5 – Zionist Party - 3 seats

List number 6 - Poalei Zion (Lyevitsa) - 1 seat
Total: 12 seats, 12 Municipal council members (radni)

The total results were:

Zionists - 5 Municipal council members
Civilian Non-partisan - 5 Municipal council members
The Jewish People's Party - 4 Municipal council members
BUND (Jewish Socialist Labor Party) - 3 Municipal council members
Individual Christian party - 1 Municipal council member
Jewish Individual Party - 1 Municipal council member
Poalei Zion - 1 Municipal council member
PPS (Polska Partia Sotsialistychna – Polish Socialist Party) - 0 Municipal council members
Jewish Popular Party - 0 Municipal council members

Education

From ancient times, Jews have paid great attention to education, which helped to preserve their language, culture, and spirituality. Due to the knowledge they received at Jewish schools, they wisely looked at the backgrounds of other nationalities. Some considered them to be cunning, but this did not detract the Jews.

In Tsarist times, Jews could send their children to Russian schools or in Poland to Polish schools, but they preferred to teach them themselves. According to reports, religious and public schools were in:
Volchin – "Talmud Torah"
Colony Sarovo, "Midrash"
Colony Abramovo, "Talmud Torah"
Ryasno – "Talmud Torah"
Verhovichi – "Midrash"
Kamenets-Litovsk "Talmud Torah Shel-Moshe," "Maryah," a Tarbut Society School, Beit Midrash, and the advanced Yeshiva, "The Talmud Knesset Beit Yitzchak." There were private teachers and about 20 children attended the Polish free public school.

Wysokie-Litovsk – "Talmud Torah" (Jewish school with 5 general education classrooms) where there were private teachers. 25 Jewish children participated in the Polish free public school until 1939. In the 1940-41 academic year, there was a Jewish secondary school.

Schools

Volchin:
A three-classroom private school "Talmud Torah" in the synagogue.
Sarovo:
A three-classroom private school "Midrash" on the synagogue premises.
Abramovo:
A two-classroom private school "Talmud Torah" in the synagogue.
Lotovo:
Children attended school in Sarovo.
Ryasno:
A two-classroom private school "Talmud Torah" in the synagogue.
Verhovichi:
A two-classroom private school "Midrash" on the synagogue premises.
Kamenets-Litovsk:
1. A two-classroom private school, "Maryah," a Tarbut Society School on Kobrynska Street (now Chkalova, Street, № 5). Now it is an apartment house.
2. A three-classroom private school, "Talmud-Torah Shel Moshe" on Shlomo Haim Gorfinkel Sądowa Street (now 40 BSSR Street 40, № 14). Now the House of Children's Creativity.
3. A private four-year comprehensive school - Beit Midrash (House of Midrash) on Podrzeczna Street (now 35 Naberezhnaya Street). Now a military registration and enlistment office.
4. An advanced private yeshiva "Talmud Beit Knesset Yitzhak" on Brzeska Street (now the House of Culture at 1 Brestskaya Street).
5. Private teachers.
6. About 20 Jewish children attended the Polish free public school.
Wysokie-Litovsk:
1. A three-classroom private school "Talmud Torah" in the Old Synagogue.

2. A six-classroom private secondary school at 24 Pocztova Street, 24 (now Kirova Street) and 32 Wyganowska Street (now Sovyetskaya Street).
3. Private teachers.
4. 25 Jewish children attended the Polish free public school.
5. Jewish secondary school in the 1940-41 academic year in a home on the site that is now the House of Culture (Testimony of teacher Nikolai Konstantinovich Manchak).

Secondary School in Wysokie-Litovsk

In 1926, the Tarbut Society received a license from the District Inspector of Education to open a five-classroom Jewish private secondary school in Wysokie-Litovsk at 24 Pocztowa Street (now Kirova Street) and at 32 Wyganowska Street (now Sovyetskaya Street). It was approved by Director Jacob Grunkart.

The teachers who taught there were Yosel Yachkovski, Eugene Braude, Morduch Kahanovich, Reeve (Rebecca) Shinder, and Eydelya Segalovich. They had to conduct classes on several subjects: languages - Yiddish, Hebrew, and Polish - mathematics, geography, history, natural history, manual skills, physical exercise, singing, and drawing. Yosel Yachkovski taught Yiddish and Hebrew.

In 1930, the Kuratorium (Department of Education) in Brest set certain conditions to be met:

1) The schools had to agree to teach the children the Polish language, at least conversational Polish;
2) The teachers had to have Polish citizenship; the schools had to adapt to the programs of the Ministry of Education of Poland;
4) There was to be mandatory compliance with the Articles of Association of the Union of Jewish Schools;
5) The language of instruction was to be Polish and Jewish (Yiddish).

At 24 Pocztowa Street, there were three classrooms (grades 1-4) and the administrative office. At 32 Wyganowska Street there was one room for grade

5. The school curriculum of classes was as follows:

Grades	Yiddish	Polish Language	Mathematics	Geography	History	Nature History	Manual Skills	Physical exercises	Singing	Drawing	Hebrew	TOTAL
I	12	-	4	-	-	-	-	4	4	-	-	24
II	6	8	4	-	-	-	-	3	2	2	2	28
III	6	6	4	2	2	2	2	2	1	2	4	33
IV	6	6	4	2	2	2	2	2	1	2	4	33
V	6	6	4	2	2	3	2	2	1	1	4	33

The teacher of the first grade was Rivka Shindler. The Yiddish and Hebrew teacher was Yosel Yachkovski.

An estimate of the school's income and expenses is:

Income	Expenses
1. Contributions from parents 7200 zlotys.	Payment of teachers 9720 zlotys (PLN).
2. Subsidies from Tarbut Society 1880 zlotys (PLN).	Rental of premises 1000 zlotys (PLN).
3. Grant from the Wysokie Magistrate 1880 zlotys (PLN).	Lighting, heating 360 zlotys (PLN).
4. Donations 700 zlotys.	Payment for the administration 500 zlotys (PLN).
Total: 11,580 zlotys (PLN = Poland).	Total: 11,580 zlotys (PLN = Poland).

It is interesting that, according to Inspector Nikolai Konstantinovich Manchak of the Wysokie-Litovsk (Vysokoye) Local Education Authority, in the 1940-41 academic year there was an advanced Jewish secondary public school where he taught.

Kamenets-Litovsk Yeshiva

Among the residents of Kamenets, the question often arose as to whether the town had a higher education institution.

At 21 Brestskaya Street, opposite the communication center, stands a modern building, the House of Culture. In the postwar period (after 1945), movies were shown there and organized dances were held. Today discos, concerts, meetings, and conferences are held there. More recently, the House of Culture has been renovated and has a modern look. It looked simpler before. Until 1939, it housed a major rabbinical school (Yeshiva). The full name of the Yeshiva was "Talmud Beit Knesset Yitzhak." It is possible to give an affirmative answer to the question asked by the people of Kamenets – there really was a higher education institution in Kamenets-Litovsk. Kamenets-Litovsk had a predominantly Jewish population. Apparently, because of this reason, this major Yeshiva was transferred from Vilna (Vilnius) to Kamenets-Litovsk in 1926. The Yeshiva was founded in 1897 in Kovno (Kaunas) and is named in memory of Rabbi Yitzhak Elhanana Spector.

The Yeshiva accepted young people ages 16 to 25 years. The basis for admission was the successful completion of an examination on which were questions about the Talmud.

Local older generation residents still remember students of the educational institution with their characteristic "side curls" ("payess"–curled sideburns) and "skull-caps" ("yarmulkas"/"kippas"), and when they spent leisure time on Saturdays and rested at the Aleksandr Mushits Garden near the Yeshiva or on the side of the Kladucha hill (Church of the Annunciation), by Shostakovsky's mill, or just walked through the streets of Kamenets-Litovsk.

Dedication of the Cornerstone of the Kamenets-Litovsk Yeshiva. 1932

Training at the Yeshiva lasted 5 to 10 years. Classes were held on average of 10 hours a day. Education was free and the students lived in private apartments. Some of the future rabbis received scholarships from funds established by various Jewish community organizations. However, many students lived hand to mouth and used a custom called "Essen Tag," which in Yiddish means "eating day." On this day, Jewish families prepared much more food to eat than usual. Once a week, a Yeshiva "bochur" (student) came to a family where he was given all the food he could eat and was able to eat his fill.

The Kamenets-Lithuania (Litovsk) Yeshiva was probably one of the largest and most famous Yeshivas throughout the province of Polesie (a territory about the size of the present Brest region). In 1938, 270 students were enrolled, including two-hundred thirty-six (236) from Poland, 7 from the United States, 17 from Germany, 1 from Italy, 2 from England, 1 from Czechoslovakia, 1 from Latvia, 5 from Denmark, and 2 from Belgium. In 1939, the total number of students at the Yeshiva reached 413. Upon graduation, certificates were issued and, on the basis of which, graduates became rabbis or took important positions among the rabbis.

The Director of the Yeshiva was Moshe Burnstein. The main teacher was Boruch Ber Leibowitz, a Gaon ("Sage"). Other teachers were Wolf Naphtali Leibowitz, Reuvain Grozovsky, and Itsko Edelstein.

Undoubtedly, Boruch Ber Leibowitz was rightfully considered the chief teacher at the Kamenets Yeshiva. He was born in Slutsk in 1866 and was a gifted young man. He even drew the attention of the Yeshiva in Volozhin. His teacher was Rabbi Chiam Soloveitchik. Boruch married the daughter of Rabbi Abraham Zimmerman. In 1904, he headed the House of Israel Synagogue's (Beit Knesset Yisroel) Yeshiva in Slabodka (a suburb of Kovno). It achieved popularity and worldwide recognition. After the outbreak of World War I, he moved the Yeshiva to Minsk and then to Kremenchug (in Ukraine). After the end of the First World War, the Yeshiva returned to Vilna, and then moved to Kamenets-Litovsk.

Boruch's quest was to rise higher and higher to the sky on Jacob's Ladder. His authority was great. When a Tarbut secular culture school was to open in Kamenets-Litovsk, he delivered a fiery speech in which he said, "We had a choice: Bereza, Kossovo, and Kamenets, and we chose Kamenets, which we cherish, but now will leave." Hearing these words, the community decided not to open a Tarbut school.

It was necessary to support the idea of Jacob's Ladder referred to above, and Boruch needed someone who would stand firmly on the ground. This man was Rabbi Raphael Reuvain Grozovsky, Boruch Ber Leibowitz's son-in-law. He was born in 1896 in Minsk into the family of Rabbi Shamshon, a leading dayan (religious judge), hence his nickname, "Reuvain Minsker." He studied at the Beit Knesset Yisroel (House of Israel Synagogue) Yeshiva in Slabodka, a suburb of Kovno. He was a gifted young person, taking after Boruch. After the outbreak of World War I, the Slabodka Yeshiva closed and the students dispersed. Reuvain went to his native Minsk, then to another city, and finally to Vilna. There, in 1919, he became the son-in-law of Boruch Ber Leibowitz. He moved, along with the Yeshiva, from Lukiški (a suburb of Vilna) to

Kamenets-Litovsk, where he was the first assistant to and the support of his teacher. Reuvain did everything to help the Kamenets Yeshiva become a large and influential institution and to allow Boruch and his family to preserve his lectures and publish them.

In his last years, Boruch was weak and gave lessons mainly at home. Twice a week, accompanied by the senior students in the Yeshiva, he went out in Kamenets where he read "Shiur" (a sermon/a lesson). Reuvain was also in the audience those days, watching everyone and everything. Boruch constantly asked students questions. For a good Dvar (interpretation) of the Torah, he gave them the prize of 10 Polish zlotys (PLN).

Boruch and Reuvain lived modestly. Their wages were minimal and did not allow for luxury. Reuvain, his wife, and their four children lived in a house. His wife's parents lived in an upstairs room in the house. The small rooms were enclosed by cardboard partitions. In three of the rooms, the partitions were covered with newspapers, but not in his room, which was plastered. He was always afraid to spend funds from the Board of Trustees Foundation for their needs. Reuvain tried to be close to his father-in-law and he would go to the stairs and invite him to come down.

The houses where Boruch and Reuvain lived with their families can be described as follows: At first they lived in a two-story house built by Yeheshkel Stempnitsky on Bialostocka Street (now 6 Lenina Street). Later it housed the Belarusbank. The house is now empty. Then they moved into a house at 2 Dojazd Street (now 10 Pogranichnaya Street) that after the war was a typography and printing business. The house is currently empty.

Reuvain Grozovsky died in America in 1956. The students of "Reb Reuvain" studied his sermons ("Shiur") at yeshivas around the world. His writings radically changed the study of Torah in America and Israel, both in everyday life and the level of learning. Reuvain was a worthy disciple of Gaon Rabbi Boruch Ber Leibowitz.

The Yeshiva had a board of trustees that was led by Boruch Leibowitz and his deputy, Itsko Edelstein. The board did not depend on the community and the Kamenets community did not help with the maintenance of the Yeshiva. The school needed a considerable amount of money. The First World War caused damage to the economy of several countries, including Poland, which was going through a difficult period in its infancy of state formation. Therefore, in the late 20s of the 20th century, Boruch Ber Leibowitz and Reuvain Grozovsky were forced to seek financial support and even went to the United States. Money began to flow into a trust fund for the Yeshiva. In 1938, the Yeshiva received money from the funds of the Professor Hofkina Foundation in Berlin (150 pounds £ - English), 15,000 zlotys (PLN - Polish) from the Yad Hayshinot Association in New York City, and 800 zlotys (PLN) from Yad Yeshivot in Vilna.

Despite the fact that the Yeshiva was a private educational institution that was independent in its activities, the Polish authorities tried to control it. A curiously interesting report from the Brest District Inspector, Edward Raducki, was sent to the Brest Kuratorium (Department of Education) in March 1938. In the report, the inspector stated that the trustee and owner of the Kamenets-Lithuania Yeshiva, Boruch Ber Leibowitz, did not know the Polish language, that the Board of Trustees of the Yeshiva's monetary fund was not registered, and that Gaon Leibowitz uncontrollably disposed of cash funds. How this ended is not known, but we must believe that everything was okay. And then, a year later, war broke out.

It is said that, in 1939, just before the war (World War II), the U.S. Embassy in Warsaw received a telegram to withdraw United States citizens who were yeshiva students. The students began to scatter all over the world. Moshe Burnstein (the Director of the Yeshiva) stayed in Kamenets-Litovsk and, in the first days of the German occupation, was executed by the Nazis. At this point, the Kamenets Yeshiva ended.

For a long time, the fate of the Yeshiva was not known. There have been several versions of the stories of the evacuation the Yeshiva. The first version is that, in 1940, some students traveled through Siberia to Vladivostok with teachers Boruch Leibowitz and Wolf Naftali Ze'ev Leibowitz. On the way, Boruch Leibowitz and some students died from the harsh conditions. Wolf Naphtali Ze'ev survived and went through Mongolia and China, and moved to

America to New York. The Yeshiva was revived in New York under the name "The Kamenets Yeshiva of America."

The second version is that after the outbreak of war in 1939, Boruch Ber Leibowitz and some students escaped to Vilnius (Vilna) and from there to America.

The third version is that Reuvain Grozovsky went to America after the outbreak of the Second World War to raise funds to feed the students who escaped from the Nazis. He was able to raise money to bring about 110 Kamenets Yeshiva students to Vilnius (Vilna), Moscow, the Far East, China, America, and Israel, where the Yeshiva opened in Jerusalem. Thirty (30) students came to New York and rest to the other places. There, on the east side of Manhattan, the Director of Kamenets Yeshiva Ketana (meaning child) was Avrahom Pinkus, former Director of the Yeshiva Torah Vodaas that has its primary offices in Brooklyn.

A recent study by Henry Neugass (from the USA) shows that it is not easy to find the Kamenets Yeshiva in New York today. The Kamenets Yeshiva was likely divided into two parts in New York, with the largest and earliest one on the east side of Manhattan and the second one somewhere in Brooklyn. At some point, the first curtailed its activities and now is a combination of a house of worship and an education center with a small number of students. Henry Neugass was able to find another Kamenets Yeshiva in Israel. Research by Jenni Buch (from Australia) showed that, after the war began in 1939, Boruch Leibowitz was able to escape with his students to Vilnius, but he fell gravely ill there and died. The teachers and students he saved organized a yeshiva in Jerusalem that is named Kamyanets (Kamenets).

Through research, Henry Neugass and Jenni Bush were able to reconstruct the events of the 1939-1940 period. After the arrival of the Red Army in September 1939, the Yeshiva students and their teachers left Kamenets-Litovsk secretly and went to Vilna (Vilnius), which had passed from Poland to Lithuania. The Yeshiva reopened there, but was forced to settle in the suburbs of Vilnius (Vilna). All of this experience was a heavy blow to Boruch

Leibowitz. He became gravely ill and died in November 1939. He is buried in Vilna.

In 1940, Lithuania became part of the Soviet Union and yeshivas were closed. A group of Kamenets Yeshiva students and their teachers, Rabbi Reuvain Grozovsky and Wolfe Naphtali Leibowitz, began their long and difficult journey abroad through Siberia. Some of the students could not withstand the hardships and died. The remaining miraculously survived and followed Rabbi Wolfe Ze'ev Naftali through Mongolia and China to the United States, where they formed an institution in New York that they called the Kamenets Yeshiva, which was designed to prepare experts in the Talmud.

Jewish Community (Kahal) Life

Historical Background

Once the first Jew settled in Kamenets-Litovsk in 1500, more Jews began to arrive. Although their number was small, about 10 people, it was enough to conduct communal prayers.

Jews began to buy land and houses and to trade. A multi-year dispute regarding the royal privilege (right/charter) to trade occurred between the Kamenets Jewish elders and their supporters and the town Magistrate of Kamenets, who represented the middle-class Christians of Kamenets. The kings had mercy on the Jews and then rained down their anger on them. They gave charters, confirmed them, then cancelled them, and gave them again. The kings needed money and, for each privilege (right/charter) or acknowledgment, the Jews had to pay. The Kamenets elders believed that all taxes that the Jews had to pay should be paid to the castle treasury (at that time in Kamenets-Litovsk, there was a castle that was the residence of the elders). The Magistrate had a different view and believed that Jews should obey the Magistrate and, consequently, pay taxes to him. The disagreement was so great that Kamenets-Litovsk received the Magdeburg Rights/Law in 1503.

Even Polish kings were arbitrators in these disputes. For example, on July

23, 1631, the Polish King Sigismund III confirmed the court ruling: "In a dispute between the warlord Krzysztof Radziwill of Brest and Kamenets, commoners' claims regarding the houses in Kamenets-Litovsk purchased by Jews should be subject to the jurisdiction of a magistrate."

Power was not always on the side of the Jews. An example of such a disfavor was the eviction in 1495 of all the Jews in Lithuania on the order of the Lithuanian Grand Duke Alexander I. However, when he became the King of Poland, he allowed them to return.

On February, 26, 1525, Kamenets-Litovsk received the right to be an urban administrative district (*wojtowstwo*) with a Vogt (*wojt*) managing the town and its surroundings. Christian townspeople obtained permits to operate taverns in the town and in its vicinity, but they rented them mostly to Jews.

The development of cities in Lithuania (not only ethnic Lithuania, but lands that were included in the Grand Duchy of Lithuania), as in other countries, led to an increase in urban population. However, in Lithuania this growth was slower than in Poland.

With the status as an urban administrative district (*wojtowstwo*), Kamenets-Litovsk was granted a municipal court.

Christian burghers in the town were vested with the legal right to keep the taverns and to evict Jews from such establishments, but that does not mean that they took away all means of livelihood from the Jewish population.

An archived document of 1565 that was compiled in order to collect taxes in the Kamenets administrative district shows, for example, the taxes that were levied: Eliezer 3 zlotys, Nahum 3 zlotys (PLN), Bichko 3 zlotys (PLN), Pesach 2 zlotys, Stopka 3 zlotys, etc. From the same document, we learn that the Jews were not only in Kamenets-Litovsk, but also in the surrounding villages.

For the first time, Jews of Kamenets are mentioned in Jewish sources (*pinkos*) in connection with the establishment of the Lithuanian Vaad (Council) that resigned from the national "Council of Four Lands."

In 1623, the Lithuanian Vaad had the power to require Lithuanian Jews to pay a certain amount of money to the Lithuanian treasury.

The Lithuanian Vaad initially consisted of three communities (Kahals): Brest (the home community), Grodno, and Minsk. Kamenets-Litovsk was unfairly overlooked. Brest, Pruzhany, Wysokie-Litovsk, and other cities held meetings of the Vaad. No meetings were held in Kamenets-Litovsk that belonged to the Brest-Litovsk Kahal.

In 1670, the Vaad, which met in Siedlce, decided to collect a community tax of 600 zlotys (PLN) from Kamenets-Litovsk. The tax was to be paid to a Mr. Yuditsky.

A historic decree was issued on December 11, 1635 by the King of Poland, Władysław IV, which was ratified in 1661 by his brother, Jan Casimir (Kazimierz), and was confirmed for the third time in 1670 by King Michael Vyshnevetsky (Michał Korybut Wiśniowiecki). The decree included very important updates for the Jews:

1. One market day per week was added, except Saturday.
2. Construction of a synagogue was authorized, with the condition that it was not to be higher or more beautiful than the local Christian church.
3. The construction of ritual baths on grounds owned by the town was authorized.
4. Jews were allowed to open a cemetery in the town or outside it.
5. Jews were allowed to engage in commerce and trade activities, and to buy property in the town and build houses.

The Christian population of the town was warned not interfere with the lives of Jews and to enable them to benefit from the rights and privileges given to them. Those that interfered with the Jews would pay a fine. If you dared to harm Jewish townspeople, you would be fined 5000 zlotys (PLN) that would be divided between the aggrieved party and the authorities.

By law, in 1629, Jews were allowed to engage in crafts and trades that did not belong to Christian guilds. This was complemented by a commercial law that allowed Jews to sell shots of vodka, wine, beer, and mead (honey wine).

It is interesting that, in 1633, King Władysław IV, referring to a decree that stated that Jewish tailors could create items only for Jewish customers, said that Jews were free to sell clothing and participate in transactions in which Christian artisans were not represented by a guild.

Hence, the Kamenets-Litovsk Jewish craftsmen were the first to have acquired the right to unlimited trade, whereas they were restricted and limited in other Lithuanian towns and places.

In Kamenets-Litovsk, as well as in Lithuania, the Jews enjoyed the support of the nobility. Note the sharp tone of Wladyslaw IV in a privilege issued to the Jews of Kamenets in 1635: "Let it be known to the administrative district of Kamenets and other urban institutions: We declare that we wish to confirm the validity of everything written in the privilege, and we command you not to violate the freedom of the Jews that was given by us."

Christian town dwellers fiercely fought the terms and conditions of the privilege. This was evidenced by a protest signed in 1693 by 40 commoners and sent to the Kamenets-Litovsk town council (Rada) against the radical Andrey Tyablevich, who had assigned the Jews the ability to tax alcoholic beverages without securing the support of other council members, exciting the whole town.

It should be emphasized that, during the reign of King John Sobieski from 1670 to 1696, the government of Poland supported the Jews as in previous years. Thus, Treasurer (Minister of Finance) Sapieha handed over the collection of taxes in Kamenets-Litovsk to Isaac Noygmovich and Yeshaya Yakubovich, both Jews. At the time, Kamenets-Litovsk was the headquarters of a branch of the Brest Customs Office that assigned the shipment of goods from Podlasie to a series of towns such as Brest, Pinsk, and Yalovka.

Disputes continued between the Kamenets-Litovsk citizens and the Jews. Once, the citizens accused the Brest Governor of complicity in aiding the Jews. The leader was Ostap Tyszkiewicz, a bee-keeper and owner of the villages of Klepachi and Pasyeki [the latter subsequently merged with Kamenets-Litovsk and became Pasieka (Apiary/Bee Farm) Street, which, in Soviet times, was renamed Levanevsky Street].

Among the documents of the town magistrate, there are those that speak of commercial relations and negotiations between peasants and Jews. Landowners and peasants from neighboring villages traded mostly with Jews, and there was no restriction about doing this. The Christian town dwellers were unhappy and dissatisfied with this.

At the beginning of the 18th century, during the reign of Augustus II, changes were felt. The commerce and economic role of Kamenets-Litovsk increased. In addition to the Kamenets-Litovsk, there was another one in the village of Klepachi, which was the property of Ostap Tyszkiewicz, whose authority extended over the whole territory adjacent to the Bialowieza Forest.

For the Jews of Lithuania and Poland, those were hard times. Frivolous accusations, slander, and fabricated charges became frequent. Various prejudices were disseminated among the Christian population. People were made to be afraid of Jewish "witches," who were alleged to have entered into a contract with evil spirits. Ordinary people heard frightening stories about Jews putting the "evil eye" on the crops.

The struggle of the Christian citizens against the Jews finally achieved its goal. They complained to Augustus II that the Charter of 1670, which allowed Kamenets-Litovsk Jews to live free; sell alcohol, honey, beer, and other beverages; conduct free trade; open shops and stalls at the market and in the town; buy and sell homes and property belonging to the nobility and the church; sell textile products wholesale and retail, as well as female small wares (e.g., ribbons, buttons, thread needles, and sewing goods); organize trades in the old town; and reduce home prices offended the citizens of Kamenets-Litovsk. In this case, there is mention of the old town. At that time Kamenets-Litovsk was divided into two parts - the old town and the new town. The western part was the old town, and included Litewska Street and its surroundings. The Jewish quarter was located in the town center and included all the lanes around the synagogue, "Der Meyer," with its religious school (Talmud Torah) and ritual bath that was located nearby.

In response to the complaint, August II ordered a ban that prohibited Jews from building houses with enclosed courtyards and trading in alcoholic beverages. He ordered the town elders to impose restrictions on Jewish commerce.

It looked like a game of "*otbivalki*" (orb/ball bouncing), if it was not life itself. The Jews appealed to the Polish kings and received charters (i.e., rights and privileges) with great effort and for large sums of money. That's why they were called at that time, "the hens that laid the golden eggs." "Golden eggs" had to be given not only to the King, but also to his office, governors, and other government officials.

In response to Jewish tradesmen receiving charters, the town dwellers sent complaints. Both parties tried to negotiate with each other and agree, but the townspeople did not accept the agreements and were disgruntled and offended and complained again.

The Magistrate of Kamenets-Litovsk was a powerful and active establishment, possessing great rights of self-government, and did not always obey the provincial authorities (*wojewodstwo*). Therefore, at times, it was necessary to apply directly to the King.

The struggle for privileges and rights between Jews and the town dwellers (burghers) carried on continuously without interruption. It was a struggle for existence.

Jewish Community Life in Kamenets-Litovsk

The Jews of Kamenets-Litovsk, if I may say so, had the Magdeburg Law or Magdeburg Rights of their own, which were partially in agreement with the town and also contrary to it. They were engaged in loansharking (i.e., charging usurious interest for loans), lesseeship (i.e., property rental agents), and crafts to a lesser degree. They had their own administration that was called the "Kahal."

The Jewish community was also referred to as "Kahal." The Kahal appeared when the towns received Magdeburg Rights (Magdeburg Law). In the towns and places where the Jewish community was small, it was attached to the nearest larger Jewish community and was called "*prikagalok*" (a sub-kahal or "under the jurisdiction of a kahal"). For example, Kamenets-Litovsk was first under the jurisdiction of the Brest Kahal and before World War II became part of the Wysokie-Litovsk Kahal.

On one hand, in terms of economy, the Kahal regulated labor and defended the material interests of members of the community (kehila). The Kahal was responsible for timely delivery of taxes to the treasury, and performed administrative tasks that were supported by the government in the management of the businesses of the Jewish population. The Kahal's power was strong and was equal to the responsibility and interests of town councils. The Kahal had wide autonomy over local community (kehila) affairs and stood watch over the morality of each of the members of the community.

The greatest power of the Kahal was vested in a board of elders – Rashim ("heads") and Tuvim ("good men") - that was elected by the local Jewish community. They made up a board with absolute power that addressed all community affairs. Each of the elders could be the leader of the Kahal and its treasurer for only one month. He was called "Ha'Parnas Ha'Chodesh" (Steward for a Month). Of lesser importance than the elders were the religious judges, trustees, and heads of the religious and educational institutions.

The head of the Kahal was a spiritual leader, the Chief Rabbi. He was appointed for six years. His contract could be extended for four years. The Chief Rabbi signed the decisions of the Kahal, supervised elections, presided over the Jewish court, imposed excommunication from the community, conducted religious rites and ceremonies, and supervised education. Any resolution of the Kahal without the signature of the Chief Rabbi was invalid.

The Chief Rabbi was the director of the Jewish school and was a "darshan" (preacher), as were the other Kahal leaders, including the clerk. All other officials were referred to as "students" as the center of community life was the synagogue and the school in it. Kahal employees included physicians, pharmacists, midwives, barbers, butchers, and others. By the way, only the Chief Rabbi and the judges received wages. The others worked for free.

However, life was not as smooth as it appeared. Jewish community life depended on the goodwill of the King that was not gratuitous or free of charge for charters, and was strewn with prohibitions and restrictions. That's how they lived.

The Jewish Community Council of Wysokie-Litovsk in 1936

As mentioned above, Kamenets-Litovsk was a member of the Kahal of Wysokie-Litovsk. It consisted of 9 representatives from the Wysokie-Litovsk, 5 representatives from Kamenets-Litovsk, 1 representative from the rural areas, and one from Volchin. There were only 16 people and one went to Argentina. The following are their names, years of birth, occupations, party affiliation, and who they represented.

Chairman:		
1. Verdun	Leib	born in 1889 - Butcher - Orthodox - Wysokie-L.
Deputy Chairman:		
1. Shatshteyn	Itsko	born in 1866 - Brick Layer - Zionist - Wysokie-L.
Members:		
1. Gelfand	Mordko	born in 1889 - Gardener - Zionist - Wysokie-L.
2. Grynszpan	David	born in 1885 - Baker - BUND - Wysokie-L.
3. Rosenbaum	Shmuel	born in 1895 - Leather Tanner - Zionist, Wysokie-L.
4. Vigutov	Yosel	born in 1870 - Merchant - Orthodox - Kamenets-L.
5. Shostakovsky	Yosel	died 12/24/1936 - Entrepreneur - Kamenets-L.

6. Berson	Moshkov	born in 1882 - Miller - Zionist – Volchin
7. Pahta Movsha	Aaron	born in 1881 - Merchant - Orthodox - Kamenets-L.
8. Bande	Chiam	born in 1889 - Butcher - Orthodox - Wysokie-L.
9. Dubiner	Moshkov	born in 1893 - Brick Layer - BUND - Wysokie-L.
10. Birenbaum	Menachem	born in 1884 - Merchant - Zionist - Wysokie-L.
11. Voyskovski	Meyer	born in 1898 - Jewish Teacher - Zionist - Wysokie-L.
12. Mikey	David	Went to Argentina.
13. Fisher	Meyer Yosel	born in 1872 - Merchant - Orthodox - Kamenets-L.
14. Gvirtsman	Itsko	born in 1865 - Merchant - Orthodox - Kamenets-L.

In 1921, the Kamenets-Litovsk Board included:

1. Pinya		
2. Stempnitsky	Abessalom	
3. Vigutov	Yosel	
4. Kozak	Tevye	
5. Viener	Moishe	
6. Kizer	Benjamin	

Kamenets-Litovsk in the Late 19th and Early 20th Centuries

At the age of 85 years, Nosazhevski, the owner of Kamenets-Litovsk, died (at that time, that is, by the end of the 19th century, the town was in private hands). After his death, Valerian Polanovski inherited the town and the remains of the former *wojtowstwo* and over time sold the surrounding farms into various private hands and urban areas to Jews. During this period, the building of Jewish houses began on the north side of the market, i.e., on part of the urban land that had previously belonged to the royal estate.

Later, Ivanov and Volginov became the owners of the town and the remnants of the administrative district (*wojtowstwo*). Volginov sold the former Royal Garden to Starks and Bigutov. After her husband's death in 1887, Volginov's wife, Maria, sold the town to Abraham Nemtsovich, a Jew from Bialystok, based on the Act of 1887 of lifelong inheritance. The last assets of the former *wojtowstwo* went into private hands before World War I. Among them were the farms that passed to his granddaughters Vnuchki, Perkovichi, Makovishche, Bryshche, and Pashuki. The town remained in the hands of Nemtsovich from whom the government bought back the rights to sell vodka on tap for 22,000 rubles.[2]

During the First World War, Kamenets-Litovsk was captured by Austrian troops that remained in the town until May 1916. Then they were replaced by German troops. On November 12, 1918, Polish troops entered the town, and in August 1920 the Red Army. However, after a few weeks, Pilsudski's Legions came back in the town. After the Treaty of Riga in 1921, Polish rule was established in Kamenets and lasted until September 1939. On September 16, 1939, the Germans arrived, and a week later the front-ranks of the Red Army appeared and Soviet power was established. With the outbreak of the First World War, and until the outbreak of the Second World War, the Jewish community of Kamenets-Litovsk endured a great deal: devastation by the military, postwar reconstruction, then a small period of peace, and then war again.

In 1915, with the arrival of enemy forces, Jewish refugees left the town and only a few Jews remained. Jews who left returned to the town after the First World War. The arrival of the Red Army and the period of German occupation will be discussed in separate chapters.

Kamenets-Litovsk in the 20th Years of the 20th Century

In 1921, the town had 2,348 inhabitants, 1,902 of whom were Jews (81%). At this time, Kamenets-Litovsk was located on 307 hectares and consisted of 39 streets and squares. One hectare included an average of 8.5 cross streets.

In 1922, Abraham Nemtsovich (Nemcovič) sold Kamenets-Litovsk and Zamosty (a suburb) for 8000 zlotys (PLN) to Isaac Yosel Gvirtsman, a Kamenets-Litovsk Jewish merchant and owner of a restaurant. He owned his new purchase until the Diet (Congress) of Poland adopted the Polish-Lithuanian Commonwealth Act, which abolished the ownership of towns and other settlements. The Polish government returned the money he spent to Gvirtsman.

The Composition of the Population of the Town by Nationality

From 1764 to 1939, Kamenets-Litovsk was inhabited mainly by representatives of four (4) nationalities: Poles, Russians, Ukrainians, and Jews. It is interesting, how the population size and nationality composition of the town varied during this period.

Year	Number of Inhabitants					Jews	Percent	Total
	Poles	Russians and Ukrainians	Total				
1764			575		866	59.2	1461
1774	600	1170	1770	Without rural areas	350	16.5	2129
1784	541	1312	1853		647	25.8	2800
1897	200	647	847		2722	76.2	3569
1921	134	312	446		1902	81.0	2348
1938	50	250	300		3500	92.1	3800
1939	70	807	877		4200	82.7	5077

If we trace the population of the town for 175 years before the outbreak of World War II, we can see that, in general, there was a steady increase in the total number of inhabitants, except for the period of 1915 to 1921, whereas the number of Poles, Russians, and Ukrainians consistently decreased, except in 1939. Starting with 1764, the number of Jews grew, with the exception of 1774 and the period from 1915 to 1921.

What was the cause of such changes in the population? There are several reasons that included the displacement of people in search of better living conditions, epidemics, wars, and fleeing as refugees. The number of Jews is not always accurate. Yehezkel Kotik's memory is that the Jews shied away from registration to avoid military recruitment of their young people during the period 1762 to 1837.

One conclusion can be drawn from these data numbers: from 1897 to 1939, Kamenets was significantly dominated by a Jewish population.

Religion, Synagogues, Cemeteries

In the life of the Jews, the spiritual development of their religion occupied a special place. Therefore, each community ("kehila") had at least one or more synagogues.

In some sources (especially modern ones), there are subtle differences regarding Jewish places of worship. Some consider subtle differences between two Polish terms "*synagoga*" and "*bożnica*" denoting a synagogue. But the building where they pray to God, be it big or small is, in fact, a temple.

Synagogues

The (Russian) Orthodox Church has several names for churches: chapel, cemetery church, church, cathedral. The Catholics call them: chapel, church, parish church, cathedral; the Lutheran's: church; the Calvinists: gathering place; the Mohammedans: mosque, Great Mosque; the Jews: synagogue, the Great Synagogue, choral synagogue.

Synagogues mainly had a simple, austere architectural form. Perhaps it began when the charter by King Jan Casimir stated: "... synagogues were not to be equal in height and beauty to churches." But sometimes Jews sought permission to build synagogues with complex architectural forms. It is possible that, because of the simplicity of architectural form, or other reasons unknown to us, most of the older synagogue buildings were not included by Soviet compilers in the "Code (List) of Monuments of History and Culture of Belarus" and were not given proper attention. What was this? Accidental forgetfulness?

Synagogues were constructed, as were (Russian) Orthodox churches, on an

East-West axis, with the entrance being on the West. Thus, the congregation in prayer faced toward the east. Separate seats were set aside for women. The synagogues were built of wood or brick.

Information gathered reveals the locations where there were synagogues. Synagogues in Sarovo and Abramovo were described in the section above entitled "Agricultural Colonies." The synagogue in Sarovo was destroyed. During the Nazi occupation, the fascist occupation forces dismantled the synagogue in Abramovo and transported it to Dmitrovichi (Dmitroviči). There was a synagogue in Ryasna (Râsna), but where it stood is not known. In Volchin (Volčine), the synagogue is now the Volchin School Workshop. It has not been possible to determine the locations of the synagogues in Verhovichi (Verhoviči) and Lotovo.

Wysokie-Litovsk had several synagogues. Two were on Wyganowsk Street (now Sovetskaya Street) near the market. One no longer exists. The building, the Great Synagogue, was newer and is partially preserved at the edge of the town near the Pulva River before Potocki Park. It is mentioned by Oleg Trusov as a monument of architecture of buildings of this type built in the 17th century. The rectangular building was constructed of brick (external and internal walls), and between the bricks there were pieces of iron and lime mortar. The walls were 1.2 meters thick. The building's height was 10 meters, its length 19 meters, and its width 14.5 meters. Inside the synagogue were four metal columns. There was a balcony adjacent to the front wall. Its dimensions were 5 meters in length and 14.5 meters in width. The eastern wall had no windows.

The north and south sides of the building had three semi-oval windows. The building's exterior was decorated by rectangular pilasters on each of the four walls. On both sides of the façade were circular turrets. Through the doorway was a spiral staircase to the balcony. On the front side, there were three small windows at the level of the balcony and two windows below. On the south and north sides of the balcony there were large windows with semi-ovals at the top as an extension of the three windows on each side of the building. The synagogue had a front door and a side door on the north side. Inside, walls separated the library and cloakroom from the main sanctuary.

After the war, the building was used as a flax storage warehouse, then a gymnasium, and the Sport Committee's Sports School from 1959 to 1967. In 1959, repairs were made and a long, narrow corridor was attached. By this time, the building had a one-story gabled roof covered with tin-plated sheet-metal.

During the repairs, the image of a menorah (a seven-branched candelabra) in dark blue paint was found under a layer of plaster.

In 1966, major repairs finally began, but eventually the Regional Commission stopped the repairs of the building, because it was not repairable. The Commission proposed to disassemble the building, but it proved to be too strong. Now only the walls remain and they are in danger of collapsing.

In Wysokie, near the Great Synagogue, was another synagogue. It was built in the early 17th century before the Great Synagogue. It was a one-story, brick building that remains on the corner of the current Ordzhonikidze Street and Kirova Street (formerly Pocztowa Street). This building now houses an auto repair shop.

Kamenets-Litovsk had six synagogues: 4 of wood and 2 of brick. They were:
1. Wooden Synagogue (Holtssinagoga in German) on Bialostocka Street (now Lenina Street), between the former branch of the Belarus Bank and the present-day Consumer Services Center;
2. Wooden synagogue "Shepshel" on Brzeska Street (now 38 Brestskaya Street);

Wooden Synagogue on Litewska Street. Pre- World War I Photo.

3. Wooden Synagogue "Kol Nidrei" on Podrzeczna Street (now Naberezhnaya Street) between the Kamenets Tower and "Der Meyer" synagogue (to the west of it on the Embankment);
4. Wooden synagogue at 10 Litewska Street (now Pivnenko Street). In 1940-1941, it was the People's Court. During the Nazi occupation, it was dismantled and transported to Białostocka Street (now Lenina Street). A

workshop was built from its wood between the branch of the Belarus Bank and the Consumer Services Center. After the war, the building belonged to the Consumer Services Center. In 2000, the building was sold, dismantled, and taken away to an unknown destination;

5. Brick synagogue combined with the Yeshiva. The building was preserved and renovated. It now is the House of Culture where meetings, conferences, performances, and concerts are held and there is a discotheque/nightclub.
6. The Great Synagogue, "Der Meyer," was preserved at the intersection of Bożnicza Street (that no longer exists) and Podrzeczna Street [now 8 Naberezhsnaya Street] as was a brick synagogue combined with a yeshiva at 21 Brest Street.

The "Kol Nidrei" and "Shepshel" synagogues, and 2 wooden synagogues, were destroyed.

The building of the Great Synagogue, "Der Meyer," was significantly rebuilt and is privately owned. It was built from the red brick, probably in the late 18th or early 19th century. Although it is not mentioned in literature known to me, as with the building of the Wysokie-Litovsk Synagogue, it obviously should be classified as an architectural monument of houses of worship (religious

Der Meyer Synagogue with Kamenets Tower. Drawn by the Author.

buildings of this type). The Synagogue's height was 8 meters, its length 17 meters, and its width 14 meters. Its design intertwined architectural elements of the Renaissance period. It was a rectangular building, with narrow doors. It lacked windows on the first floor, except for the facade on which there were two small windows. There were three windows with a late Baroque look on the north, south, and west sides on the level of the second-floor balcony, adjacent to the front. The building was situated on an east-west axis, the entrance being from the west. A wooden staircase to access the balcony was located on the north side inside the front door. The roof was two-storied and covered with shingles. The Synagogue is clearly seen in the drawings by Napoleon Orda in the late 19th century.

The Great Synagogue introduced the so-called "nine-field" style. In the middle of the hall, in the center (ninth space/square), framed by four metal columns, rose the bimah (like a Christian pulpit). It was located on the east-west axis, and was enclosed by a small cast-metal fence. On this elevated platform, the solemn reading of the Torah and the study of excerpts from Holy Scripture occurred. In the eastern part of the synagogue was the Holy of Holies - the Ark of the synagogue ("Aron Kodesh"), an altar cabinet where the Torah scrolls are kept. The Aron Kodesh was topped with carvings and the Tablets of the Covenant on which were engraved the Ten Commandments. It was the most beautiful place in the Great Synagogue, decorated with numerous details and biblical characters. The altar cabinet was built in a special niche that was hidden from prying eyes with an ornate curtain.

Entry View - Der Meyer Synagogue. Pre-World War I Photo.

The synagogue was lit by low hanging lamps with fancy shapes.

The unique solemnity of prayers gave the Synagogue a splendid grandeur. The decorations for the Torah scrolls were made of silver and precious stones. There were silver bowls, incense boxes, lights, menorahs (seven-branched candlesticks), cups for washing hands, a "*chuppah*" (a canopy for wedding ceremonies), and a "shofar" (ram's horn), which was sounded on the holiday of Rosh Hashanah, the Jewish New Year.

Only men sat in the main hall. The women sat in the balcony.

On the front pediment of the Great Synagogue was the inscription: "Oh, what fear this place evokes! For this is none other than the house of God." Two lamps lit the entrance. The pediment was decorated with pilasters and three Stars of David. The name "Great Synagogue" was given to the main, most important synagogues. It is no accident that "Der Meyer" was named this. Not far from the Synagogue were Market Square and a concentration of Jewish homes, shops, and stores.

The area where the Synagogue was located was bordered by Market Square and Kobrynska, Brzeska, and Peretsa Streets, as determined according to religious law in the Psalm: "From the depths I appeal to you, Lord!"

The Synagogue was open on Saturday and on major religious and national holidays. In Tsarist times, there were prayers for the welfare of reigning rulers. In the interwar period, on the occasion of Poland national holidays, such as May 3 and November 11, the Synagogue held a solemn service for the well-being of the Marshall and President of the Polish Republic.

Before "Shabbat" (the Sabbath), there was a symbolic fencing to protect the Jewish streets in the Synagogue's area. Fences were installed on the east side to provide a sense of calm and peace-of-mind while praying. The Synagogue, in addition to being a house of prayer, was a place for learning Holy Scripture. Jewish homes, shops, stores, and markets concentrated around the Synagogue made an integrated community that created an economic center for the Jewish community. It was also the site of meetings, celebrations, and weddings.

The Great Synagogue building survived, but in the reconstruction era after the war it was a starch factory, a cash register machine company, and "Raduga" and "Troika" shops. The building is now owned by a farmer.

Cantor Yaffe

On the night of Yom Kippur (The Day of Atonement), the synagogue overflowed. Brightly lit hanging lamps and wax candles burned, casting dark, deep shadows. Along the Eastern wall of the synagogue were the old men of the town dressed in white robes. They slowly swayed like trees in the forest and muttered prayers. Then silence reigned, and everyone held their breath, waiting for the start of the singing of "Kol Nidrei."

Notable people of the town also came to listen, and stood there with an expression of awe and reverence on their faces as the strains of "Kol Nidrei" were sung by the town's cantor, Cantor Hesker Yaffe, and the choir. All present were filled with reverence and felt the approach of the Day of Reckoning.

It is difficult to convey in words the impression produced on those present by the sweet, exciting, soulful singing of Cantor Hesker Yaffe, a short man with long gray hair, who was endowed with many talents. He painted signs for shop owners, studied, was trained in the law, and, of course, was the town's cantor. Although neither he nor any of the local young people that sang in the choir had studied at a conservatory, they all knew how to sing the notes smoothly. Whenever one of the singers made the slightest mistake, one glance from the Cantor was enough to fix it at once. Cantor Yaffe not only had a powerful, strong voice, he was an excellent interpreter of Jewish prayers. Even those who did not understand the words of the prayers could easily grasp their meaning. How could one forget his prayer for rain ("Rainfall"), and his other compositions - real gems! They caused delight for everyone who heard them.

This is how the faithful stood on the evening of Yom Kippur and enjoyed listening to the sole-stirring prayers.

On that day, hardly anyone could be found streets. There was complete silence in the whole town. The chanting of prayers in synagogues could be heard. The prayer of "Neilah," which completed the service on the Day of Atonement, was said by the Cantor with sincere feeling. Every word was an expression of sadness and prayer. Was this not the last hour when the fate of each person will be irrevocably decided? But as soon as the Cantor stretched out his hands to heaven and cried in a strong voice: "Open the gates for the day is almost gone!" all in the synagogue believed that the gates of heaven really opened and the prayers of the worshippers were accepted. With a lightened heart, the worshipers murmured the phrase: "Next year in Jerusalem!" And so the Yom Kippur service in the town came to an end.

Looking back on those bygone times, and those Jews who are no longer there, you realize how many talented people in the town were killed, and how great their achievements would have been if they lived in other places and under different circumstances.

Kamenets has moved on and Jews and synagogues are no longer there. How can we forget them? It was a whole era!

Cemeteries

A cemetery is the necropolis (burial ground) for those who left us to another world. It connects the world of the dead with the world of the living. In Jewish cemeteries, the graves were marked with tombstones that first had inscriptions in Hebrew and later in Yiddish. In the old days, tombstones were made of cut stone, and then they were manufactured in Kamenets out of sandstone, which knowledgeable people said was mined somewhere near Siemiatycze. Tombstones were done in patterns of synagogues, tents, and havens of the Lord.

Not all of the settlements where Jews lived had a Jewish cemetery. There were no cemeteries in Lotovo, Sarovo, and Abramovo. Jews in those settlements buried their dead in Kamenets-Litovsk. It has not been possible to establish the location of a Jewish cemetery in Verhovichi. There was a Jewish cemetery in Volchin, but its location is unknown. In Ryasno, according to a resident of the village, Antonina Plisun, the Jewish cemetery was located north of the market place, on the other side of the Kamenets-Wysokie Highway. A resident of Wysokie-Litovsk, Anna Musevich, said of the Jewish cemetery in Wysokie-Litovsk: "It was on the hill, east of the current House of Culture, opposite the mill on Wyganowski Street (now Sovetskaya Street)." Another Jewish cemetery was recently discovered in Wysokie-Litovsk by the director of a local college, Yuri Saharchuk. It is located at the exit from Wysokie-Litovsk on Lumna near the current agricultural college.

Kamenets-Litovsk had three Jewish cemeteries:

1) The oldest was on Brzeska Street, where a branch of the Agroprombank (Agricultural Bank) stands, as reported by an inhabitant of Kamenets-Litovsk, Yaroslav Mushits;
2) The old cemetery, "Kvores," dating from the 18th century, started from Brzeska Street (now Matrosov Street), with houses surrounding it. It extended southeast to northwest from Brzeska Street to Paseka Street (now Levanevsky Street);
3) The new cemetery was located 200 meters from Szossowa Street (now 8-go Marta/8th of March Street) in a wooded area near the Sanitary Devices Installation Specialists organization.

There no longer are any Jewish cemeteries. All traces of them have been wiped out. There are no tombstones. They were used as sharpening and grinding stones, for paving roads, and for stairs.

Tombstones Found

In May 1997, I was telephoned by the head teacher (now Director) of the Kamenets Grammar School, Natalia Doshchik (after marriage Pototskaya), who said that the steps near the old Polish school were being dismantled. I immediately went there and saw mangled stairs and tombstones from Jewish cemeteries. I knew about them before. I wrote about this twice in the local newspaper, but there has been no response or answer from the authorities.

In front of the school there were 6 whole tombstones and 13 pieces of broken ones. I called a newspaper photographer and he took 2 pictures, a general view of the slabs and a close-up of them. I got on my bicycle and rode to the Deputy Chairman of the District Executive Committee, N.I. Voytsik, and told him everything. He offered to move the gravestones to a specific location. He ordered them transported into the courtyard of the landscaping unit of the Department of Education. After a while, I went to the landscaping unit and found 6 whole tombstones and 37 pieces. They were in disarray. I wrote to the newspaper again. After that, all of the whole tombstones and pieces were stacked neatly in one place.

The tombstones were rectangular and 95 cm. high and 50 cm. wide. I told the workers that they had not removed all of the tombstones and that a few more were under a layer of asphalt.

Children who gathered around the tombstones showed genuine interest. I told them about the history of old Kamenets, and about the Jews and their cemeteries and tombstones. One boy had a camera and took a few pictures of the tombstones. Student interest was high. Two girls, Sasha Romadina and Raya Parafenyuk, and other students even came to my house and asked that I tell them again and more about what I told them near the school, which I did. Interest was high. The children asked questions and listened carefully to my story.

A few years ago, asphalt near the grammar school (formerly the old Polish school) was removed and, as I said earlier, there were more gravestones. These five tombstones marked the northern side of the Kamenets Secondary School No. 1. I visited them several times, but one day discovered no tombstones. They had disappeared somewhere. I wrote to Alla Kovaleva, a journalist at the regional newspaper, Zarya (Dawn), about the Kamenets tombstones, but have not received a reply.

In 1999, to the right of the branch of the Belarus Bank on Brestkkaya Street, I found four granite slabs from the old "Kvores" cemetery with Hebrew inscriptions. With the help of a photographer that was invited, color photographs were taken. I wanted the tombstones transferred to the water conservation zone near the water tower. Public utility workers from the landscaping department promised to help, but they did not keep their word. In the meantime, a parking lot has been constructed and the tombstones were covered with sand.

Kvores Cemetery
Tombstone - Photo
by A. Karagoda. 2000

It was good that pictures were taken and have been made. Thanks to the help of Irit Abramsky, a Doctor of History from Yad Vashem in Jerusalem who was in Brest at the International School of the Holocaust, it was possible to find out what was written on the gravestones. The first inscription was: "Here lies (is buried) our teacher Rabbi Abraham

Yitzchok son of Moshe Joseph, 1925." A second tombstone's inscription was "Here is buried Rabbi Zeev Abraham."

Hopefully, the tombstones from Kamenets will find their rightful place.

It seemed that the subject was over and done, but it was not. A person from the Wysokie, Yuri Saharchuk, reported that more tombstones were recently discovered there. In May 2008, during a regional seminar for librarians, I introduced the audience to my work, "A Repository of Knowledge" (about Kamenets area libraries). I asked the librarian of the village of Shcherbovo near Kamenets, and she said that a fragment of a slab had been found with an inscription in an unknown language. I realized that it was a fragment of a Jewish tombstone and advised her to keep it and to photograph it.

Rabbis and Cantors of Kamenets-Litovsk

1. Leibowitz	Baruch Ber	Rabbi, Sage, the story of his fate is controversial
2. Grozovsky	Reuvain	Rabbi, Sage
3. Leibowitz	Ze'ev Naftali Wolfe	Rabbi, Sage
4. Burstein	Reuven	Rabbi, Director of Kamenets Yeshiva, shot by the Germans in 1941
5. Gorfinkel	Shlomo Chiam	Rabbi, Director of the Talmud Torah Shel-Moshe, shot by the Germans in 1941
6. Yeshua	Yitzchak	Rabbi, judge in matters of religion (a "dayan")
7. Golobchik	Shmuel	Rabbi, judge in matters of religion (a "dayan")
8. Rosenstock	David	Rabbi, judge in matters of religion (a "dayan")
9. Leiser	Velvel	Rabbi, judge in matters of religion (a "dayan")
10. Stempnitsky	David	Rabbi
11. Tymyanski	Yisrael	Rabbi
12. Ashkenazi	Yeshua	Rabbi, "mohel" (performer of circumcisions)

13. Simkhovich	Zymel	Rabbi, "schochet" (slaughterer of kosher meat)
14. Soroka	Joseph	Rabbi, "schochet" (slaughterer of kosher meat)
15. Tsymel	Shlomo	Rabbi, "schochet" (slaughterer of kosher meat)
16. Abraham	Ze'ev	Rabbi, was buried in a grave near the Belarus Bank
17. Abraham	Yitzchak	Rabbi, teacher, son of Moshe Joseph, was buried in a grave near the Belarus Bank
18. Rogoznitski	Elizer	Rabbi, teacher
19. Sapirshteyn	Asher	Rabbi, teacher
20. Sapirshteyn	Shlomke	Rabbi, teacher
21. Sapirshteyn	Hershl	Rabbi, teacher
22. Alter	Velvel	Rabbi, teacher
23. Kirshenbaum	Velvel	Rabbi, teacher
24. Rappaport	Piña	Rabbi, teacher
25. Sapirshteyn	Velvel	Rabbi, teacher
26. Terk	Yosel	Rabbi, teacher
27. Rudnitsky	Shlomo Lisker	Cantor
28. Yaffe	Hesker	Cantor

We can assume that there were more. However, bad times came to Kamenets-Litovsk and it does not seem possible to recover the names of all of the rabbis and cantors.

Jewish Culture in Kamenets-Litovsk

Kamenets-Litovsk was once an important town in the Grand Duchy of Lithuania, but after incorporation into the Russian Empire in 1795, it became a provincial town. It seemed that it would be a "backwater" town in the "middle of nowhere," with no development of cultural life. Actually, it turned out otherwise. In Kamenets-Litovsk, cultural life did not let up. There were working libraries. Debates were held, there were literary evenings, and acting in theatrical circles. Professional artists came and the firefighters' brass band played. The town's residents chose a Jewish spiritual elite of "wise men," writers, poets, and teachers. There were working Jewish schools and a yeshiva. The latter especially supported the fertile minds of the Kamenets community.

Libraries

Since ancient times, people have needed information to increase their knowledge. Information is contained in manuscripts and books and the manuscripts and books had to be stored and maintained in a specific place. This place became known as a library.

In Kamenets-Litovsk, the Jews had their own private libraries, in which there were Jewish and world classics in the Yiddish language:

1) Children's Library (720 volumes);
2) The Peretz Library (1014 volumes);
3) The Sholom Aleichem Library (1248 volumes).

These libraries were popular and were maintained by the Kahal and voluntary donations. The Yeshiva also had its library in a room on the second floor, where books in Hebrew were kept. "Sage" Baruch Ber Leibowitz had his personal library of 450 volumes of religious books in Hebrew.

The Peretz Library had a wide selection of books in Yiddish. Young people had become engrossed in reading the Jewish classics of Peretz, Shalom Aleichem, Sholom Asch, Avrom Reyzen, and others. They were interested in the works of literary critics Baal-Mahashavot, Asher, and Trinka. They also read the works of world literature and the classics that were translated into Yiddish.

During evening walks in the summer, the youth discussed and shared their opinions about the books they read.

In a building on Dolina Street (now Proletarskaya Street), the Peretz Library often arranged for readings in the evening. Anyone who would like to ask a question wrote it on a piece of paper and placed it in a special box. The organizers read the questions and asked if anyone present knew the answer.

Those present answered the questions based on their knowledge. Then there were lively debates. Thus, it was kind of a collective learning experience.

Literary evenings were organized. Passages and excerpts from books were read and analyzed, and yielded a critical evaluation of literary works. Thus, the library was a source of knowledge that everyone could receive.

Cultural life was not avoided by political parties. The Zionist Organization, which had headquarters in a house on Podrzeczna Street (now Naberezhnaya Street), collected money for the Jewish National Fund. The Fund organized literary evenings with visiting artists on Saturdays. An example was the event dedicated to the trial in the Shakespearean work "Shylock." The hall was overcrowded and it was stuffy, but there was complete silence when Lipa Horowitz read the play. Those present followed the process of the trial with interest and listened carefully to the arguments by the prosecution and the defense.

A significant role in acquiring new knowledge was by reading newspapers. The choice of newspapers was quite large, "Unser Polesie Express" (Our Polesie Express) (Brest), "Polesie Shtime" (Polesie Voice) (Brest), "Polesie Nayes" (Polesie News) (Brest), "Unsere Veg" (Our Way) (Lvov), "Haynt" (Today) (Warsaw), "Kobriner Shtime" (Kobrin Voice) (Kobrin), "Pinsker Tribune" (Pinsk), "Pinsker Leben" (Pinsk Life) (Pinsk), "Pinsker Vort" (Pinsk Word) (Pinsk), and others. Usually, a few people subscribed to one or another newspaper, and the copies were passed from hand to hand.

Amateur Theater

Speaking of culture and education, one cannot help but remember the four Sapirshteyn brothers (Asher, Shlomke, Herschel, and Velvel) who were known throughout the entire town. They were private teachers, and each of them taught their own subject. Asher taught children in his home on Krutka Street. But they were famous primarily as amateur artists and organizers of drama circles. The big amateur theater was directed by Asher Sapirshteyn. He produced well-known plays, such as "The Sale of Joseph," "Shulamith" (the heroine of the Song of Solomon), and others. His three brothers, Velvel,

Herschel, and Shlomke, and his wife Zelda, were the main actors. Shlomke and Zelda played the roles of Isaac Vlender and Sarah Rudnicki very well. In addition to these well-known plays, Asher put on the operetta "Bewitched." The actors were young boys and girls. Sender played the role of the sorcerer. Diklinga, who played the role of the apprentice tailor, sang beautifully. Maya Goldes, a charming girl, appeared in the role of Babkeleh and played the role and sang beautifully. The operetta was successfully performed multiple times. The audience received it warmly and ardently applauded the actors.

Undoubtedly, theatrical activities contributed greatly to the cultural life of the town. Additionally, amateur theatrical companies often toured in Kamenets-Litovsk, especially during the holidays of Shavuot and Sukkot. Due to the lack of special facilities, performances were conducted in a barn of Motie Klepacher or a big house on Dolina Street (now Proletarskaya Street).

Writers and Poets

Kamenets-Litovsk was awarded a great honor when an outstanding writer, Yehezkel (Ezekiel) Kotik, was born into a large family in April 1847. Like all Jewish children under 17 years, he studied the Talmud, but he did not choose the path to become a rabbi. Within two years after he married, he owned land in different villages.

Young Kotik went to the big city - Kiev. However, his arrival coincided with a period of anti-Jewish pogroms. This prompted him to leave Kiev and to move to Warsaw. There acquired the Café on Nalewki Street, which for many years was a meeting place for Jewish writers and activists in the labor movement.

His principal occupation was to engage in public affairs. He founded a number of philanthropic societies and institutions. At that time, he also became engaged in literary pursuits. He printed pamphlets in Yiddish and Hebrew, and published a book of short stories. But international fame came to him from his memoirs, "Mayne Zikhroynes" ("My Remembrances"), published in two volumes.

Of particular interest is the first volume, in which the author, using his family as an example, gives a vivid picture of Jewish life in Russia in the middle of the 19th century. In the book, he describes the social, political, and cultural relations of the time. In addition to its cultural and historical value, "Mayne Zikhroynes" has literary value. Characters that appear in the pages of the book are described very vividly.

The Kamenets-born Jewish writer, Yehezkel (Ezekiel) Kotik, died in Warsaw in 1921.

It is hardly possible to speak about the creativity of Yehezkel (Ezekiel) Kotik better than was said by the classic Jewish writer, Sholom Aleichem.

In a letter to Kotik in January 1913, from Lausanne, Switzerland, he wrote: "...I started reading your 'Remembrances' and what can I say? I cannot remember when I experienced such great pleasure and spiritual delight! This is not a book, it a treasure, a garden, a paradise full of flowers and singing birds...Your book almost made me crazy! Who is this Kotik? I've heard about someone whose name, I think, is Kotik, who is a young Jew with a grey beard. What fascinated me about your book is its sacred, simple truth, and genuine simplicity. And the language! No, you not only are a good, honest, faithful guardian of a rich, enormously rich treasure, you have a talent from God and don't know that you have the soul of artist. Many Jews were in Kamenets and Zamosty. As you say, you had many relatives in your noisy family. But why did none of them gather the memories together like you do? Why has not one of them shown imagination like your imagination, which burns as a flame?

"Will you continue to write your 'Remembrances'? Will they be as rich and masterful as the first volume? Masterful? I'm sure they will be. But will they be rich? I do not know. I am afraid that their content would be poorer and leaner, because there are no more Jews! That is to say, they are there, but not so evident. They are like a drop in the ocean, especially in large towns.

"Why is our book market flooded with worthless junk and a treasure such as yours is packed in boxes, crates, and under tables and mattresses. A terrible hatred grows in me against our critics whenever I remember how they praise every young scribbler who creates an obscenity...

"Are you still writing your Remembrances? During what time period and about whom do you write? Is it going smoothly as before? Do you write about your family? There are people and characters whose stories you should continue to tell.

"Live long, be healthy and happy, and write! Your thankful reader, friend, and pupil,
Sholom Aleichem."

What do they know about Kotik in his native Kamenets? Nothing, or almost nothing, except for a small article I published in the local newspaper, "Kamyanyechchyny News," in 2000. His book, "Mayne Zikhroynes" (My Remembrances), is not even in the Kamenets Library named after Ignatovski.

There were other writers in Kamenets-Litovsk, but they were less known. In addition to his direct duties, Moshe Burnstein, the director of the Yeshiva of Kamenets-Litovsk, was engaged in literary work. He wrote books and also went to sell them in North America. As reported in the "Chronicle of Jewish Life in Kamenets-Litovsk," the well-known wealthy man, Yosel Gvirtsman, bought the entire town of Kamenets-Litovsk in 1921, but was compelled to return his acquisition to the state by a decision of the Polish government. Unfortunately, Burnstein's works were not published anywhere else. And, in the days of the terrible war, all traces of them have disappeared.

During the interwar period, a little-known poet named Hirsh Kreisky lived in Kamenets-Litovsk. This is not to say that his works of verse were insignificant. No, his poems are good. I could judge this because, after the war, I held and read a hand-written manuscript of a book of his poetry.

When the Nazis perpetrated the Holocaust of the Jews of Kamenets, the Jewish poet, Hirsh Kreisky, threw his book of poems from a convoy. Krystyna, the wife of the Commandant of the Fire Brigade, Franèk Jakubowski, picked up the book and kept it. After her death, her daughter,

Jakubowska (after marriage Kieskiewicz), showed me the book. I found that the poems in the book were written in Polish in 1918-1923 in Mogilev-Podolsky, Lviv (Lvov), and Bydgoszcz. After Adela's death, the book went to her heirs and all traces of it have disappeared.

It would be remiss not to mention another poet, Moses Teitelbaum, who was born in Wysokie-Litovsk. He wrote his poems in Yiddish and published them in the Jewish press. He was on friendly terms with the Polish painter of Wysokie-Litovsk, Józef Charyton, who dedicated his work to the Jews and the Holocaust.

Scholars

The Kamenets Yeshiva was distinguished from other similar institutions of its kind, because it and its students were capable of continuing in the absence of the chief teacher in creative courses that were built over 40 years. The main teacher was Boruch Ber Leibowitz, who is remembered with love in the Jewish world, and is regarded as the greatest Talmudic expert of our time. Boruch's basic principle of teaching was that the study of the Talmud and related subjects should be conducted for the benefit of the students themselves, not for material remuneration. Thus, the Kamenets Yeshiva not only prepared rabbis and other clerics, it was engaged in research and scholarly pursuits. The anthology published by the Kamenets Yeshiva, "Deggel Naftali," contains the original research and reflections of the scholars about the most abstruse rabbinic problems.

Leisure Time

In their time off from work and on holidays, the Jewish population of Kamenets-Litovsk took evening walks along the Brzeska Street, Kobrynska Street, (now Chkalov Street), and Białostocka Street (now Pogranichnaya Street) in the direction of the bridges across the Lesnaya River (there were three bridges).

Walking on Saturday night and on holidays was a tradition. Everyone wore their best clothes. Married couples, lovers, students from the Yeshiva, and boys and girls strolled. Some talked quietly and others loudly, trying to get their companions to agree with their arguments. The subjects of their conversations were literature, politics, and world and local events.

In the spring, on both sides of the river, yellow marsh marigolds ("*kachintsy*") appeared. They covered the meadows, flood plain, and forest, transforming them into a golden carpet that was pleasing to the eye.

On summer days, the young people loved to ride in boats, while singing songs to the accompaniment of a guitar.

This went on for many generations. Today only the mind can reconstruct that old, distant Kamenets, the Kamenets that no longer exists. Actually, it does exist, but it is quite different.

Yehezkel Kotik on Kamenets-Litovsk

No one can better tell about the old Kamenets-Litovsk in the 19th century than the Kamenets writer Yehezkel Kotik, who loved and remembered his native land all of his life. Let's listen to some excerpts from his memoirs:

"... Kamenets consisted of 280 small, old, blackened houses with steep roofs. The number of "souls" (i.e., residents) recorded in the Russian State Registry was 450. In this regard, a logical question comes to mind. Two hundred and fifty homes compared with only 450 "souls"? How is that possible? The answer is very simple. Prior to 1874, when the new conscription (recruiting) law came into force, two thirds of the Jews were not registered. The government actually knew about this virtually all of the time, but did not intervene and remained silent about it. It was only in 1874, after the Tsar issued a decree that those who were not registered would not be punished if they signed up, did all of the "missing" begin to register. Government commissions traveled across the country from one town and village to another, registering the "missing."

"It was very interesting that, in those past years, four hundred and fifty souls of my town that were registered had to provide a prescribed number of recruits for military service. At 30 km. (kilometers) from Kamenets is the small town, Wysokie. Its official registration book noted about 550 "souls." All this time Wysokie and Kamenets jointly produced a set of recruits. The soldiers were recruited on the basis of certain rules; for example, one soldier per thousand inhabitants. The population of Kamenets and Wysokie were to provide one soldier for Tsar Nicholas I each year. Based on its population, Kamenets was to provide less than half of a soldier, and Wysokie a little more than half of a soldier. This presented a challenging problem. Finally, it was decided in the following way: Kamenets provided a recruit one year and Wysokie one the next year. Once every ten years, Kamenets was exempt from providing a recruit. The calculation was simple and took into account the difference in the number of residents in the two small towns. After the mutual agreement about recruiting was reached, soldiers for the army were recruited in this way until conscription was abolished.

"...As usual, the market had two rows of shops. A lane passed between the two rows, and it was so narrow that a horse-drawn cart could hardly pass. Three or four shops sold high-quality fabrics. The customers were Jews and the surrounding rural landowners. Three or four of the merchants sold aprons, scarves, clothing, and more. Others sold dry goods (haberdashery), pitch (resin), coal tar, and others.

"Only women and teen-age girls sold in the shops. They sat opposite each other, excited, and flushed. Of course, there also were girls and married women helpers who successfully attracted prospective customers into stores, especially those from the villages, calling to them with loud voices.

"But the 'higher class' customers, Jews and the landowners, had their specific shopkeepers and no one tried to forcibly pull those consumers over to their side. Such a customer was perhaps quietly accompanied by a curse, which would also be directed at the saleswoman that sold him the goods.

"Actually, the turnover (sale of goods) was quite small, except on Sundays, because, on the other days of the week, the peasants rarely came to town. Therefore, the women sat idly in front of the shops and were bored. However, Sunday was market day and a large number of people came from the villages. They crowded and pushed near the doors of the shops, buzzing like flies on a window sill sprinkled with powdered sugar.

"Important institutions of the town were taverns that were fairly numerous. The peasants could eat cheese, herring, and cucumbers there, and there was also a large quantity of alcoholic beverages. Only members of the gentry and nobility and the owners of small estates could afford other pleasures. After they drank, they were not satisfied, as were the peasants, with slices of cheese or herring, and they also ate pieces of goose and fish. These taverns, just like the shops, were run by women. Only on Sundays, when business was brisk and there was a large turnover, did the menfolk also help.

"How did the men occupy themselves? They also did not sit idly by. In the vicinity of Kamenets there were several hundred estate owners. They each had several hundred or even more serfs (peasants). The serfs worked and sweated day and night, but remained poor. On the other hand, the owners of the estates clearly enjoyed life. Each of them dealt with one or two Jews in town who benefitted from the landowners to a greater to a lesser extent. If a landowner had two Jews in his entourage, one of them was referred to as a "good Jew" and was a respected merchant. The other was less prominent regarding his outward appearance and the respectability of his commercial dealings. Both Jews were considered trustees and authorized representatives of the landowner. The "good Jew" helped him more with advice, the other was a "Jack of all trades" and his role was more ambiguous. Both, however, lived in great fear of their patron. Although they earned wages and the landlord acted as their defender in dealing with the authorities, nevertheless, we should thank God several times a day that this type of relationship with the landowner has disappeared. If the landowner took it into his head, he could severely beat the Jew, and then tell him, "If you keep quiet, you'll stay with me. If not, I'll employ another Jew, and you cannot do anything to me, because both the magistrate and the chief of police are my friends." The Jew silently thought, "I was beaten. This is because he is the landowner. On the other hand, I eat my piece of bread because of him. When I close my eyes forever, my child will be making a living from him." His reflections were quite correct. When the Jew serving the landowner died, the landowner took on in his place his son or son-in-law, whoever was more pleasant. It was like a marriage contract and the Jew received the landowner as a kind of inheritance.

"Perhaps it's worth noting here that the landowner also had his own craftsman in the town to which he gave all of his work. In the town there were various craftsmen: shoemakers, tailors, tinsmiths, and others. It is clear that it was more difficult for them to make a living than for the owners of the shops. Although rents were low, they had to pay ten or twelve rubles a year for a flat. They could not afford to live by themselves in an apartment and a small house was shared by two or three families.

"In those days, the tax assessor and the district chief of police were the real rulers of the town. When there was a quarrel between Jews, they immediately turned to the tax assessor, appearing before him accompanied by their wives, children, friends, and relatives. The assessor judged in favor of the person who gave him a large sum of money or aroused the most sympathy in him. If one of the parties challenged the decision and filed a complaint against the assessor with the district police officer in Brest, it was rarely effective. On the contrary, the bold man was not worth a half-penny afterwards, because the assessor could persecute him and even beat him before arresting him. As a rule, the district police officer went hand in glove with the assessor.

"At that time, the district police officer exercised full authority in the region. The notions people had about the provincial governor were indeed strange. He was considered as being at the same level as the Tsar, and no one would ever conceive of the idea of involving him in Jewish affairs.

"The Governor lived on his rural estate and was the authorized representative of the Tsar. Also, he had a tenant, usually a Jew. And when he had several estates and villages, a trustee and a tenant also lived there. It is clear that the Jews trembled with fear of the Governor, when at that time landlords could punish peasants, men and women, and the young and the old over trifles. What impact could a little Jew have?

"You can imagine how a trustee (a factotum), lessee, and their children lived in constant fear of the estate owner. And if they had a pretty daughter, life turned into a terrible disaster. They feared that the daughter might attract the attention of the owner, because he had the power to do anything he wanted. Pretty Jewish village girls always looked dirty, unwashed, and covered with soot and grime so their good looks went unnoticed. Only when the girls went into the town, and after they washed with soap and water, did the people recognize that a village Jew had a pretty daughter.

"The landowners hired Jews that conducted the majority of the owners' affairs. The landowners believed that a Jew was clever and cunning, yet honest. Each landowner believed that only his Jew was honest, and that the rest were thieves and swindlers. Jews were sent on errands to his colleagues, other landowners. Although landowners had Christian managers, who ran the estate and gave orders to the peasants, they preferred to deal with the Jews.

"The majority of estate owners that lived around Kamenets were not very rich (did not live lavishly). The soil of the Kamenets area was marginally productive. The crop from one "morgen" of land (0.56 hectares) was not more than four shocks of sheaves (60 bundles of grain). Each shock yielded about 5 to 6 carts of corn. Little wheat was grown in the Kamenets region. Here and there were plots of fertile land of a dozen kilometers and there the crop yield per acre was 18 to 20 shocks of sheaves.

"The landowners, who lived 15 to 20 km. from one another, often held balls, each time on the estate of another landowner. These celebrations were grand, with the best wines stockpiled for the occasion. In fact, these balls led many landowners into financial difficulty, so they never had enough money.

"Jews typically bought grain, alcoholic beverages, and wool from the landowners to sell. Payment of a large sum of money was made in advance and frequently exceeded the cost of the goods that were purchased.

"It was enough for merchants to run to the landowner and to try to get the prices offered to regular customers reduced. Nevertheless, those goods that the landowner wanted for himself, he purchased from an "exclusive" Jew, with whom no one could compete.

"The Jews constantly reassured their wives that the landowners were not bad people and that they could earn money from them. Only when there was an 'evil moment' did everything become bad. Apparently it came from God. 'When God wants to punish me, he sends a crazy idea into the landlord's head. Let atonement put an end to my troubles and may God help to protect me.'"

The Terrible 20th Century

In place of the relatively calm 19th century, came the terrible 20th century, with its devastating wars. First, the Russo-Japanese War, but it was far away in the Far East. Then wars came close to our place. The First World War, refugee status, and deportation, when people were forcibly resettled in the interior of Russia. It was a disaster, but the big disaster was ahead. People enjoyed a peaceful respite, but gradually they grasped the warning. There, far to the West, the muffled sounds of cannons firing and bombs exploding were heard. The war was coming nearer. September 1, 1939 was the outbreak of World War II and its terrible consequences.

Kamenets-Litovsk was dealt with in stages. On September 16, 1939, German soldiers came. They behaved calmly and properly with the people. These were not the Nazi murderers that appeared two years later.

A week later, the Germans left Kamenets-Litovsk. On September 25, 1939, the Red Army troops entered the town. New procedures were established and it changed the traditional way of life.

The Arrival of the Red Army

Did the people of Kamenets expect a new, modern government with the appearance of the Red Army? Yes, they expected and waited, as usual, for the fulfillment of their hopes for something new. Did their hopes come true? What did the people expect from the new government? The unemployed expected work, the peasants expected new plots of land, the members of the underground expected new positions, and the poor expected the privileges of wealth. Affluent people weighed staying away. Polish intellectuals, retired soldiers and officers of the Polish army, officials, and landowners reacted to the new government with hostility, and the new authorities did not favor them. The underground came out of hiding and put on red headbands, representing the civilian militia, and expropriated the property of landlords and rich people. Throughout the year, mass deportations to Siberia and Kazakhstan began of those people that the new authorities considered to be hostile. A person authorized to deport named Kozhuro said, "We will get rid of all of you, masters' henchmen."

With the arrival of the Red Army (i.e., the Soviet Army), the situation for the Jewish population changed for the worse. Local Jewish Communists, who were in the underground, Leiser Dolinsky, Joseph Volfson, Joseph Abraham Kupchik, the Yakobson brothers from Zamosty, Malka Radish, and other members of the the Communist Party of Western Belarus, occupied decision-making posts. And since they were very familiar with each resident of the town, they knew who, and to what extent, to support and nominate.

At that time, more than half of the Jews of Kamenets lived through trading and selling various goods in their stores and shops. With the new government, they lost their source of income and livelihood. Soon the stores (stalls) and shops were closed and were taken away (nationalized) from the Jews. Starting business operations came to be called "speculation." The Soviet authorities nationalized everything that could be nationalized: the mill, power plant, vegetable oil production, the brewery, the distillery, brick and tile factories, the carbonated water plant, etc. Most of the houses were also nationalized. The family of Dora Galperin was evicted from their home. The Galperins were forced to live in someone's apartment. The synagogue was closed and the Yeshiva was turned into a club and a movie theater. All Jews had to work on Saturdays and Jewish holidays. It was a strong attack on the religious beliefs of the Jews. In 1940, in Kamenets-Litovsk and Wysokie-Litovsk, rows of stalls were demolished and in their place parks were laid out. In the same year, Kamenets-Litovsk and Wysokie-Litovsk were renamed simply Kamenets and Wysokie.

War!

I remember June 22, 1941. My father (he directed the schoolboys' choir) had to go to Minsk for the national review of amateur performances. I was awakened by my grandmother who said, "Wake up my grandson, it's the war!" I was awake in a flash. I saw an unforgettable picture. In the East, the sun has not yet risen, but the sky had already turned pink and the whole western horizon was bluish black. I heard thunder, but it was not thunder. It was shells being fired. Soon, low flying ominous birds began flying low, but they were not birds. German aircraft were flying eastward.

In Kamenets, war began tragically. At dawn, from somewhere in the distance, two heavy shells flew from very long-range guns. One exploded outside the town in a swamp near Tsyganska Tonya, ("*tonya*" is a very deep creek in the Lesnaya River). The second exploded on Bożnicza Street behind the "Der Meyer" synagogue. Debris struck the wall of a Jewish home and one of the fragments killed a Jewish woman who was sleeping. She was the first victim of World War II in Kamenets. At 10:00 a.m. German motorcyclists were in the town. These were not the peaceable German soldiers that the people saw in September 1939. These were the killers.

The First Executions of Jews

The arrival of the Germans in Kamenets marked the beginning of executions of Jews. Here is what eyewitnesses said.

Dora Galperin: "I myself saw them catch David Rosenberg's son-in-law, who came from Zamosty. The murderers brutally beat him, punched him, and kicked him with their boots." (06/22/1941)

Adelina Grushevskaya: "On the first day of the arrival of the Germans, seven Soviet citizens (seven Jews) were shot near our apartment on Novo Senatorska Street." (06/22/1941).

In the first days of occupation, the Nazis shot and killed the Director of the

Yeshiva, Reuven Burstein, and Gorfinkel, the Director of Talmud Torah Shel Moshe.

From the account by Dora Galperin of events in Kamenets in 1941: "Before the war, a doctor's nurse, Galina Vaydenberg, lived in Kamenets-Litovsk. She suddenly disappeared. We found that the Germans took her and killed her because the postman, a Christian, told them that she received letters and postcards written in Yiddish."

"... Miriam Pashter-Vapnyarska lived next door to Reyzel Gvirtsman. The Germans occupied her home on Białostocka Street. Previously, she had hidden something in the garden. When she got there and tried to dig it up, a policeman ran after her. The policeman began to brutally beat her and then shot her."

"... Sister-in-law of Reyzel Gvirtsman went mad from fear of the Nazi killers. She once left home and did not return. It turned out that the Germans caught her and shot her."

After single murders, the Nazis switched to mass executions. In July 1941, as told by Vasyl Troychuk of Komarovshchina, the Germans staged a raid (round-up) in Kamenets and shot more than 100 Jewish men by the *vodomy* (gully) on a tract of land called "Rovets," which is near Bolshye (Big) Muriny, two kilometers from the town and left of the Kamenets-Brest Road. There was a mass grave. Birch trees grew and then died. The place was then plowed. Now, there is a solitary tree growing there. (The account was written on 11/18/1997. The witness died in 2004.)

Eyewitness Paul Gorbatsevich, who spoke Yiddish well, said, "In June 1941, the Germans in Kamenets-Litovsk rounded up about 120 Jewish men. My father and I were working in a field near Rovets. We saw a car drive up and heard shots. Jews were executed at Rovets located near Bolshye (Big) Muriny, near the Brest Highway." (Recorded on 11/18/1997. The witness died in 2005.)

As a witness, Andrei Potoka said, "In the month of July 1941, 108 Jewish males from the local population of Kamenets-Litovsk were taken in vehicles to the Muriny field, two kilometers from the town on the Brest highway. There they were shot at Rovets." (The witness has died. The testimony was recorded on March 17, 1945 and is contained in "Acts of Atrocities by the Nazi Invaders in the District of Kamenets.")

The Removal of Jews from Pruzhany and Their Return

First, the Nazis decided to put the Kamenets Jews in the ghetto in Pruzhany, but there were difficulties with the placement. They abandoned the plan and allowed the Jews to return to Kamenets-Litovsk.

Here's what Marat Botvinnik wrote in "Monuments of the Genocide in Brest": "In the autumn of 1941, the Nazis decided to put the population of Kamenets in the Pruzhany ghetto, but after 2-3 weeks individual families returned to their homes."

Marat Botvinnik is not entirely accurate. Kamenets Jews were not taken to the Pruzhany ghetto in the autumn of 1941 and in August of the same year.

Here is what Andrei Potoka, a resident of Kamenets said…"in the fall of 1941, the entire Jewish population of the town of Kamenets, about five thousand people, was taken to Pruzhany. After two to three weeks, individual families returned to Kamenets." His testimony was recorded March 17, 1945 and is contained in the "Acts of Atrocities By the Nazi Invaders in the District of Kamenets." Andrei Potoka did not accurately determine the time of the removal of the Jews in Kamenets or their number. The exact time of the removal of the Jews from Kamenets to Pruzhany was recalled by the Kamenets witness, Paul Gorbatsevich: "In August 1941, the Germans removed the Kamenets Jews to a ghetto in Pruzhany. After two to three weeks, individual families retuned to Kamenets by walking." (Recorded on 11/18/1997. The witness died in 2005.)

The Ghetto in Kamenets

After the Jews of Kamenets returned to the town, construction of the ghetto began. First, there were two ghettos that then became one. Their construction was carried out slowly, with a particular intent.

Marat Botvinnik wrote: "All returning Kamenets Jews were herded into a concentration camp ghetto. It was located in the area of Brzeska, Kobrynska, and Litewska Streets, between the present day hospital and the store located on the Litewska Street (now Pivnenko Street)." (From the book "Monuments of the Genocide in Brest Region.")

The newspaper "Leninets" on October 7, 1992 published, "The ghetto was surrounded by a fence and barbed wire."

A resident of Kamenets, Andrei Potoka, said, "For the Jewish people returning from Pruzhany, the Germans had arranged for them to be settled in the Kamenets town ghetto. A part of the town was surrounded by a fence entwined with barbed wire. Communication with the rest of the town was ceased. In the area of the ghetto, the entire population had only one well and there was not enough water and food."

From the account of Vasyl Troychuk from Komarovshchina: "The ghetto was located near the Tower along the south side of Podrzeczna Street, to the east of the butcher's house, from Litewska Street up to Smocza Street, along Kobrynska Street, up to the hospital; a plot between Market Square, Brzeska Street, Polna Street up to the priest's house." (Recorded on 11/18/1997. The witness died in 2004.)

The Nazis methodically prepared the Holocaust of the Kamenets Jews. They forced them to wear a distinctive sign sewn on their clothes, a yellow patch. Then, yellow stars were nailed on the houses where Jews lived. For better control of the occupants after the return of the Jews to Kamenets from Pruzhany in the autumn, a ghetto began to be constructed. For management of the Jewish community, the Nazis created a *Judenrat* with an unarmed Jewish police force, the task of which was to keep police-like order in the ghetto. The occupants constructed the ghetto slowly. From time to time, through the *Judenrat*, a contribution of gold for the suspension of building the ghetto was imposed by the Nazis. Then the construction continued again.

This was repeated several times. There were cases of Nazis coming to Jewish homes and taking away furniture, clothes, and other belongings.

Initially there were two ghettos. The first was a small one in the area of Asha Street, Brzeska (Brestkaya) Street, Gleboka Street (that no longer exists), Targowa Street (that no longer exists), and Polna Street (now Gogolya Street). The second, a bigger one, was in the area of Kobrynska Street (now Belova Street), Litewska Street (now Pivnenko Street), Malaya Street (no longer exists), Smocza (no longer exists), Krutka (no longer exists), Podrzeczna Street (now Naberezhnaya Street), Wąska (now Sryednyaya Street), Bożnicza Street (no longer exists), and Zamkowa Street (no longer exists). By January 1, 1942, there was one large ghetto. It began from the Tower on Zamkowa Street and went along Podrzeczna Street (the south side of Naberezhnaya Street) up to the butcher's house; along Litewska Street (now Pivnenko Street, the south side) to Smocza Street (it does not exist now); along Kobrynska Street (now Belova Street, the north side), including the streets Mala, Krutka (no longer exists), and Wąska Street (Sryednyaya Street).

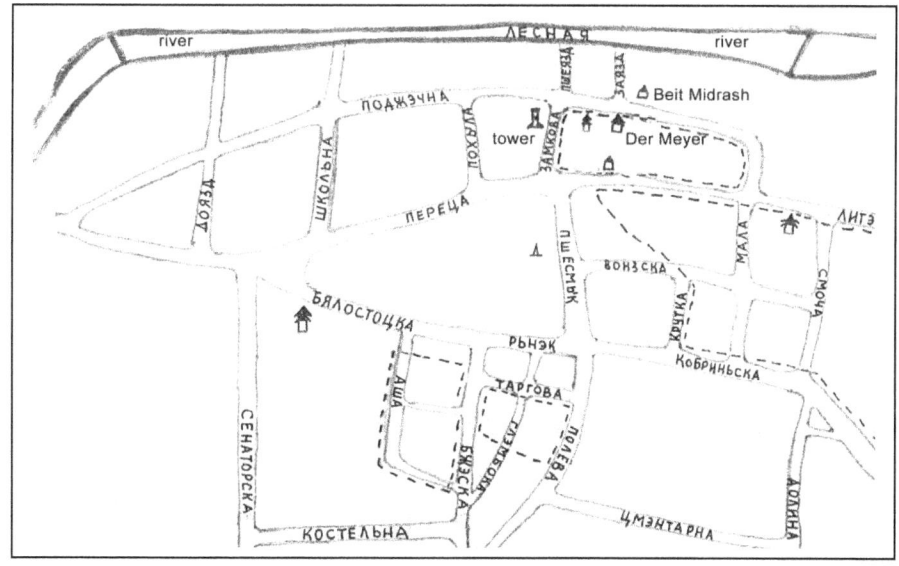

Diagram of the Kamenets Ghetto. Drawn by the Author. Street names are in Russian.

The ghetto was surrounded by a 2.6 meter barbed-wire fence with three gates on Kobrynska Street (now Chkalova Street), Litewska Street (now Pivnenko Street), and near the *Judenrat* (now the library at Lenina Street). Every 10 to 20 meters around the ghetto were poles with electric lanterns that were lit from evening to morning.

Initially, security was carried out by the local police. Some police officers stood at the gates in shifts, while others made systematic patrols of the ghetto. Occasionally, patrols were performed by paramilitary police officers from the Kamenets police. Then security was intensified by visiting police officers.

At first, when the ghetto was not yet fully constructed, many people went to town and bought food. Then the ghetto was locked down and it became worse. There were negligible amounts of products granted to them through the *Judenrat*. They lived hand to mouth with hunger and starvation. Living conditions were very difficult. The ghetto had one well. In Jewish homes, 10 or more people often lived in one room. Overcrowding was terrible and unsanitary conditions prevailed.

Nevertheless, despite the approaching tragedy, life in the Kamenets ghetto continued as did life in the Bialystok ghetto. That's what a participant in the Bialystok ghetto, Voronezh University Professor Simon Byorkner, who I met with, told me: "People even tried to live an ordinary life in the ghetto; they rejoiced, mourned, loved, and gave birth. Poets wrote poetry verses and there was a theatre. A Jewish resistance group operated in Bialystok and resisted as best as they could."

There were instances of escapes from the Kamenets ghetto. A large group of Jews escaped, but seeing the hopelessness of their situation, came back through the *Judenrat*. A Jewish escapee, Pinya, was extradited to the Germans by the *sołtys* (headman) of the village Bolshye (Big) Muriny. The well-known doctor, Noah Golberg, went into hiding with his son Hirsch, his daughter, Janeczka, and his son-in-law, Ludwig, who was Polish. They hid in a shed on the *khutor* (farmstead) Smuga near Dmitrovichi, but were given up to the Germans by a local policeman named Garah from the village of Osinniki.

First and foremost, the Nazis hated Jews, but they also hated other people as part of their fascist ideology.

The Executions Continued

The Nazis continued to shoot people after the creation of the ghetto. The events of 1942 tell us:

Vladimir Zhitinets from the village of Bolshye (Big) Muriny: "...I was familiar with some Jews. I cannot forget Pinya and his wife Rachel. Pinya was a wonderful carpenter and his wife worked in a tavern. They were good, worthy people. When the Jews were being hunted down, Pinya went into hiding for two weeks. He then wanted to visit his family, but there was a round-up and he was almost caught and barely escaped. He then hid in the back of the old brick factory near Muriny. The officials of the village gave up Pinya to the Germans and the fugitive likely was shot."

Dora Galperin: "The mother of Simcha Dubiner ran through the garden adjacent to Litewska Street. She wanted to give some food to her son. A German shot her. She was still alive and trying to get up, muttering her last words, 'Woe is me!' The killer shot and killed her. A few minutes later, there were more casualties. The victims were Velvel Issachar Frazer, the son-in-law of Zina Porolski, and people from Warsaw, guests of Dr. Golberg." (Also killed at that time was Frazer's daughter, Bella).

When the Jews were taken out of the colony of Abramovo to the Bialystok ghetto in 1941, a Jew fled and hid in the woods. In the spring of 1942, people found him hung from a tree.

Michael Mamus of the village of Kamenyuki: "Golberg was a remarkable doctor. He handled cases where the disease could not be handled by other doctors. He saved my brother from death and cured him. When the Nazis herded the Jews into the Kamenets ghetto, he and his family went into hiding on farms. Only his wife remained in the ghetto, and there went insane. The policeman, Garah, gave up their hiding place to the Germans. The Nazis shot them all: the doctor, his son, Hirsh, his daughter, Janeczka, and his son-in-law, Ludwig. Their common grave is near the Dmitrovichi on the edge of the forest on the right side of the Kamenets-Kamenyuki road. His brother came from Minsk every year and laid flowers on the grave." (The Golberg family was shot in 1942.)

Michael Korolyuk from the village of Svinevo: "We hid a Jewish family in our house for a few weeks. Then they left. The Germans caught them and shot them. Their burial place is unknown."

On page 205 of the book "Memory" of the Kamenets District, George Parafenyuk writes: "According to local residents B. Brishchuk, P. Zhuk, V. Zhitnits, and V. Pylypchuk, there probably are Jewish graves on the territory of the village council (village Soviet) of Rataychitsy, in particular in the Verkhovichi Forest outside of the small village of Kustychi."

Gary Kardychkin testified that, in 1942, in the forest near Kustychi by the Wysokie-Vidomlya Road, the Nazis executed the Jews from the village of Lishnya: Motya Altman, Moishe Altman, Lydia Altman, Sarah Altman, Chiam Altman, Velvel Shapiro, David Shapiro, Basya Shapiro, Abraham Shapiro, Pasha Shapiro, Gitl Shapiro, Yoselya Shapiro, Beykesh Shapiro, and Beyla Shapiro, and from the village of Leshanka, Shane Shapiro. Their burial place is unknown.

The Wysokie artist and photographer, Józef Charyton, witnessed the terrible events of 1942 in Wysokie, and wrote: "One night I heard the stutter of a machine gun. At dawn, I saw several dead bodies under my windows. It turned out that the same thing happened in different parts of the town. Looking about and orienting myself to the situation, I felt the fear of imminent destruction. The Jews, en masse, attempted escapes through weak spots in the fence, but the weaknesses in the ghetto had been zeroed in on by the Nazi machine guns."

A document in the State Archives of Brest Region (f-514; op.-1; d-41, p.-17) states: "In 1942, three kilometers from Chernavchitsy, in the village of Malaya (Small) Turna (on the border of the Brest and Kamenets Districts), about 200 Jewish men from neighboring villages were brought there and shot dead. Their grave is unmarked."

The book "Final Solution of the Jewish Question in the Western Regions of Belarus" (Minsk, 2000, page 129) states that "...in the spring of 1942...140 members of the Jewish population of Vidomlya in the Kamenets District were executed..." This is a mistake, because 140 Jews never lived in Vidomlya. The shootings by the Nazis took place at a tract of land called "Rovets" near Bolshye (Big) Muriny. Jews from Bolshaya (Big) Turna, Vidomlya, and Kamenets were executed there.

Here is what a resident of Vidomlya, Gary Kardychkin, testified: "At a tract of land called 'Rovets,' the Nazis executed Shlomo Dolinsky and Tsiva Dolinsky from the village of Vidomlya and villagers from Bolshaya (Big) Turna, including Gedalia Gvirts, Leib Gvirts, Zoellick Gvirts, Luba Gvirts, Mirko Gvirts, Ziehl Gvirts, Yankel Ebertana, Lyuba Ebertana, Hirsch Ebertana, and Leila Ebertana.

Taken from the village of Vidomlya to the Pruzhany ghetto were Chava Dolinsky, Hirsch Dolinsky, Itka Dolinsky, Yosel Dolinsky, and Moishe Dolinsky. From Vidomlya, the Nazis took Litman Dolinsky to Volchin and executed him. From Baranki, Vihnesa Galovsky, Chiam Galovsky, and Lazer Galovsky were taken to the Kamenets ghetto."

A resident of Bolshye (Big) Muriny, Vladimir Zhitenets, said, "On a day in late May or early June 1942 at 10 o'clock in the morning, 140 Jews from the Kamenets ghetto were brought to a tract of land called 'Rovets.' All of the inhabitants of Muriny who were in the village heard the stuttering of machine gun fire. The women of the village cried and made the sign of the cross (crossed themselves). At that time, no one could approach that place. It was cordoned off with barking dogs. And then the *soltys* (village headman) ordered that those that were shot be sprinkled with more ground, saying that the warmth could result in a contagious infection. Previously, birch trees grew there, but no longer. The place is not designated by anything. Only a solitary tree grows there. Perhaps, the bones of the residents still lie near the tree in the rye field."

Gregory Zaretsky of Sarovo colony said that Sarovo Jews were taken by the Nazis to the Kamenets ghetto where they shared the fate of the Kamenets Jews: "Eliezer Ashkenazi, Joseph Sokolowsky, Herschel Zaydinger, Moishe Zimovich, Yisrael Kravetski, Schlemu Chorny, Yisrael Ashkenazi, Herschel Lichtser-Kustin, Velvel Lichtser-Kustin, Moishe Yosel Lichtser-Kustin, Mordechi Simovic, Chaim Chorny, Joseph Soroko, David Zaydinger, Shimshelya Zaydinger, Lieb Kustin, Bobel Kustin, Froim Kustin, Yankel Kustin, and their wives and children."[3]

The Nazis killed the Jews of Chernavchitsy, Volchin, and some villages, as evidenced by a document in the public archives of Brest (f-614, op.-1 d-41, p.-17): "At the end of 1942, 350 Jews from Chernavchitsy were taken in to Volchin (Wołczyn) and were executed there." The book "Memory" of the Kamenets District told it this way: "On the northern outskirts of the village of Volchin, 395 Jews who were residents of the villages of Volchin and Chernavchitsy were the victims of Fascism." This happened in late October 1942. There is a concrete monument there, but with a red star. This is the only place in the Kamenets District where there is a monument for the Jews killed by the Nazis.[4]

The artist from Wysokie mentioned earlier, Józef Charyton, recalled: "At the end of February 1942, after the closing of the ghetto in Wysokie, a number of Jews were hiding for a short time in hiding places that had been prepared. They were discovered and were executed on the spot. Then, captured Jews were detained in a synagogue (that was located by the riverside near the Great Synagogue on the outskirts of Wysokie) and in groups of some dozens were led away and shot behind a leather tanning shop that was not far."

Vladimir Yefimovich Volodin wrote on page 197 of the "Memorial Book": "The civilian population of Wysokie was killed by the Nazis in a sandy area near the village of Ogorodniki. More than 40 people were taken from Wysokie (Vysokoye) to a concentration camp and, on May 22, 1942, they were killed." One must understand, according to Volodin, the Jews were innocent, peaceful civilians. The Nazis closed the Wysokie (Vysokoye) ghetto in late January 1942 so the Germans could not have killed the Jews in the month of May. They must have done this much earlier. The Nazis conducted more executions in another place - Vulka Tokarska. Like in the preceding locations, except Volchin, there are no memorial signs of the executions of the Jews, and I'm not speaking of monuments.

When the Jews from Kamenets were led to the Wysokie ghetto, those who were exhausted and lagged were killed on the road by the Nazis. It is almost impossible to establish where they were killed by the enemy monsters.

The last executions by firing squad occurred in March 1944. The Chairman of the Belaya Village Council, I. Mogilatova, drew up the Act on Crimes Committed by the Nazis: "…in the woods in March 1944, the enemy occupiers also killed a lieutenant of the Kolpak detachment, who was born in 1921, and another partisan, whose name is unknown, and 2 Jewish families, totaling 9 persons: Mzyar – 7 souls, Srul – 2 souls." (Author's Note: There are errors in the grammar of the Act and they have not been corrected.) The commander of the partisan detachment, or more correctly "division," was not Kolpak, but rather Kovpak. The Jewish families apparently lagged behind the partisan formations. We assume that the shootings occurred in a forest somewhere between Chvirki and Belaya. The exact place of the executions and burial is unknown.

The Story of Dora Galperin

The only surviving victims of the Holocaust from Kamenets that I know of for certain are Leon Gedalia Goldring and Dora, the daughter of Moshe Aaron Galperin, owner of the hotel. They alone survived. Leon endured the horrors of Auschwitz. Dora endured suffering during the years of occupation, hiding from the Nazi murderers. She described her experiences in her memoirs that cannot be read without emotion.

Terrible Days and Years

It was only the beginning. In 1940, the Communists, without any reason, threw the Galperin family out of their home. Dora's sister, Reyzel, went to live with a restaurateur, Bronek Szydlowski, and Dora went to live with a Kamenets townsman, Fyodor Panasevich. The war began. The Germans came. He immediately said he would not hang a yellow star on his house that meant that Jews lived there. After this ultimatum, Dora went to live with Reyzel Gvirtsman. She saw how the Germans caught Jews on the street and severely beat them, and then murdered David Rosenberg's brother-in-law from Zamosty. When the occupation forces opened fire on a large group of Jewish men outside of the town, everyone became intensely fearful.

Once, two gendarmes (police officers) came to the Gvirtsman house. They took almost everything, even the curtains, blankets, and furniture. As if that was not enough, they put an old hat on Reyzel's head and a big pot on Dora's and forced them to dance. Then, as if that was not enough, they removed their belts and brutally beat the poor women. They added injury to insult.

It became known that the Nazis took away a pre-war nurse, Galina Vaydenberg, confiscated all of her belongings, and shot her to death.

Dora was a witness as the Germans beat and then killed Miriam Pashter-Vapnyarski.

All this was depressing to the psyche of Jews of Kamenets. They felt an indescribable terror, expecting that an unknown tragedy would occur.

The Ghetto

When they opened the ghetto, everyone thought that there would be changes for the better. But changes for the better did not occur. On the contrary, everyday life in the ghetto worsened. A tremendous overcrowding of people living in the houses in the ghetto was created. There was a shortage of food and water. Every day the Germans made new demands. They themselves did not enter the ghetto and operated it through the *Judenrat*, a Jewish Council appointed by the Germans.

At first, the ghetto was not closed. You could go out into the town. One day, Dora went into town to buy food for her sister's children. She was stopped by a policeman and was severely beaten. She fell. The policeman did not calm down and repeatedly kicked her in the stomach with his hobnailed boots and continued the beating. This happened outside the ghetto. The severity of the beating can be judged from the fact that her face remained swollen for two weeks. After this incident, Dora tried to not leave the ghetto.

The murder of Jews continued. Dora's sister-in-law, Reyzel Gvirtsman, could not bear such a life and went insane. One day she left the house. The Germans caught her and shot her.

On January 1, 1942, the small and large ghettos were combined into one large ghetto. Dora, her sisters, with Reyzel Gvirtsman's family, moved into the large ghetto. It was no better there and the suffering increased. The Nazis continued their bloody business. Early the next morning, they killed Simcha Dubiner's mother on Litewska Street. A good man, a Christian, Mitya Kozlowski, found her and carried the body of the murdered woman to the Jewish cemetery and buried her there.

On the same day, at the same place, Issachar Velvel Frazer, his daughter, Bela, son-in-law of Zina Porolskoy, and Dr. Golberg's guest from Warsaw were killed. The doctor himself, his son, daughter, and her husband managed to escape from the ghetto and hid, but they were given up to the Germans by a local police officer and they were all shot to death. Golberg's wife, who stayed behind the barbed wire, went mad.

Dora spent three days in the large ghetto. Release from the ghetto came on the third day.

Courage and Escape from the Clutches of Killers and Suffering

At noon on the third day, Juzek Golach, a sausage maker by profession and a cheerful person who liked taking big risks in life and knew Dora, went to the barbed wire and tried to persuade her to escape. To dispel any doubts, he said that there were no Germans around and that the guard was only the local police, with whom there was an agreement that they would look the other way. Golach then left for some time and then returned with a close friend (*kumpel*) of his. They came with an axe, which they used to cut the wooden boards in the fence and pulled her out of the ghetto. Nearby, a woman by the name of Kozlovskaya was waiting. She wrapped Dora in a blanket and took her into the attic of her house.

From Kozlovskaya's house, Dora was taken to a Lithuanian Christian, Yuzik Grigorevskomu. His wife was so frightened of having to be accountable to the Germans that she took their children and ran away from home. Doubt crept into Dora's mind about whether she would be able to escape from the ghetto or would have to go back. In the evening, her doubts were dispelled when another Christian named Nicholai Zhuk came with a cart and took her to a farmstead (*khutor*) where there were only two houses. During the move, Dora was paralyzed with fear. She thought that the Germans would catch them, but nothing happened and they reached the farmstead safely. The new location was comfortable. However, the homeowner began locking her in the barn for the whole day. She came into the house briefly in the evening and then, once again, hid in her hiding place.

Once Zhuk went to Kamenets and came back and told Dora that the ghetto had been dismantled and that all of the Jews had been taken to Wysokie. She realized that it was the end of her kinsmen. She felt sadness and despair and cried incessantly, but crying did not help. Her host became more anxious and upset.

She came into the house only briefly in the evening and then, once again, hid in her hiding place. She spent six weeks this way. One morning, when she decided to enter into house, she saw Germans arriving in a motor vehicle. Her life this time, as in other instances, literally hung by a thread. Instinctively, she ran out of the room and quickly climbed to the attic.

The Nazis spent a whole day in the house, and Dora sat in her clothes in the attic in fear that the Germans would catch her, and that she would be tortured and killed. When the Germans left, her host came to take her from the attic, but she was so scared and so cold that she could not walk independently.

Zhuk carried her down from the attic in his arms. The visit from the Nazis scared her host's entire family incredibly, and he took an unhappy Dora to Kamenets that night.

Events unfolded as in a detective novel. People who wanted to save her came forward, even a local police officer, who lived with his mother on Litewska Street. He had seen Dora escape from the ghetto and agreed to hide her. She spent seven months in hiding there. They put up a curtain behind a stove and she stayed there and listened to conversations in Russian by neighbors coming into the home. Her hosts became increasingly anxious about their lives if the Germans found a Jew in the house. It was necessary for Dora to change her accommodations. Mrs. K. (Kozlovskaya) then took Dora to her house. However, the house had no place in which to hide. In addition, Dora learned that that Mrs. K.'s son intended to kill Dora in her sleep and throw her into the river. After she found out about it, a person who lived on the same street (Litewska Street) took her to his house during the night. After a while, Dora moved to a girlfriend of Mrs. Kozlovskaya, who lived in a lane near Litewska Street. It was a place where she could be well hidden, but it did not last long, because a German family moved in. The idea of committing suicide never entered Dora's mind. Evidently, her fate was to stay alive and tell you about the incredibly difficult life under the Nazis.

Living in a house where there was a German family became dangerous. Dora had to once again change her hiding place, especially because people began to say that, before retreating, the Germans would burn Kamenets. She had to hide again, this time with the sister of Nicholai Zhuk in village of Uglyany. She hid in a hole where potatoes were stored. It was damp and dark and she had to lie crouched over the entire time, but it did not last long. The front line was approaching and cannon fire could be heard in the distance.

In July 1944, the Germans withdrew. Soviet reconnaissance agents appeared before this, but it was not announced. The agents left and again danger was present. As Dora came into the kitchen, the German occupiers broke into the house, without any regard. (Author's Note: looking for Soviet spies.) Unable to find them, they left. These Germans were the last. Dora remained in the village for several days and then returned to Kamenets.

Release

On July 22, 1944, the last living Jew from Kamenets returned to her hometown. Her feet ached terribly and her legs were swollen, because of the two years she spent in the absence of fresh air and in the cold and mud. During this time, she lived on a razor's edge in constant fear for her life.

In Kamenets, she saw a quiet, deserted town. It seemed that even everlasting rocks emitted tears for those people who left into eternity. So much blood of innocent people was shed here!

Dora's appearance in the town was greeted by the local people in two ways, good and bad. She found it difficult be in Kamenets and felt that she was in danger. She went to Brest, hoping to have the right there like everyone else to live and breathe free. But Dora was mistaken.

Out of the Frying Pan and Into the Fire

One day, two men knocked on the window of the house in Brest where Dora lived and asked who lived in the house. They demanded that she open the door. When she did, they drew their pistols and pointed them at her. Then they opened the cupboards and took everything. When she asked that they leave a coat, one of them shot over her head. She dropped down in fear. They ordered her not to leave the house for 20 minutes or else they would open fire. Apparently, they were bandits that at the time flooded the city.

Dora learned that there were arrests in Kamenets. People were informing on one another to the authorities. People with whom she lived after the Germans came and expelled her from her home began scheming against her. They were afraid of possible retaliation and involved their relatives in the scheming.

Once some people from the Soviet KGB came to Dora and asked about Volodya Grigorevsky. What Dora had to do with Volodya can be found in the Author's Comments at the end of this saga.

In a Soviet Prison

Dora was arrested in October 1944. A Major from the State Security Police (KGB) interrogated Dora, and maliciously repeated the question as to why the Germans allowed her to live, as if he wanted her dead. He beat her twice and shouted that she was not telling the truth. Every night Dora was taken for questioning and was severely beaten. Some days she was kept in darkness, and she was given only one slice of bread for food. Again she fell into despair.

At one point during the interview, she saw "the witnesses" against her in her case, a cousin of the already known P. and his sister-in-law, Anyuta (Annie). Anyuta shamelessly lied that Dora was not hiding from the Germans, was the mistress of the *Kommissar* (i.e., the highest German rank of the Nazi occupation administration in the town or village) lived well, and even changed her hairstyle. Anyuta acted on the principle that the more improbable a lie is, the more plausible it is. The enraged interrogator then took off his shoe and hit Dora on the head with it and poured ink from an inkwell on her.[5]

Dora was very sick for the six weeks she was in a prison cell. She could only lie on the hard, damp floor.

Court

At the end of her sixth week in the Soviet prison, the trial took place. In the courtroom, with an exhausted Dora, were the most dangerous criminals and five security guards.

A three-judge military tribunal sat in judgment. There were 12 witnesses in the hall. Dora was completely exhausted. They called the first witness. He told the tribunal that everything he knew about her was recorded in the minutes of the investigation. One of the judges said to him, "What is written in the minutes is none of your business!" and added, "Your duty is to tell the court everything." The witness was silent. Another judge asked Dora if she wanted to speak. Dora asked the witness, "Did you see me after the Jews were taken from the ghetto and did you know that I was alive?" To this question the witness responded unequivocally, "No." The same answer came from other witnesses. Only Annie (Anyuta) still tried to cast aspersions on her, but the prosecutor interrupted her and said, "Are you perhaps angry that Dora was left alive?" Thus the basis of the indictment and the investigation collapsed. I must say that the tribunal judged objectively and held those witnesses who gave false testimony accountable, including Annie, who was arrested for perjury. With regard to Dora, the tribunal stated, "Released from custody in the courtroom." Justice prevailed!

Back to Prison

The joy was short-lived. For some unknown reason, Dora was retained in custody. It still took quite a long time before Dora became really free.

She was detained for almost a year, although she was found innocent by the court. She was kept in a small basement with 45 people, suffering from the cold, hunger, and thirst.

The End of the Story

On September 13, 1945, Dora indeed became free. She was released from imprisonment. Confused, she went out on the street and did not know where to go. She had no lodging and no clothes, except for what was on her that had turned into rags during her year of being incarcerated. Like a newsreel, the scenes and events of the Kamenets ghetto and what happened afterwards flashed before her eyes. Dora felt that she should leave this region where so much Jewish blood had been shed as soon as possible.

She was alone and for a long time and could not decide where to go, but still felt that was necessary to go. She found a girlfriend and went to Poland with her. There she fell ill from hunger and felt pain and unhappiness. Due to gangrene, she had two operations to amputate two toes on her left foot. Gangrene was the result of the inhumane living conditions under the Nazis and her stay in the horrible Soviet prison.

Author's Comments

In her memoirs, Dora Galperin did not name the people who helped her hide from the Nazis, but only indicated their initials or the first letter of their last names. The names are now known. The person with whom she lived for some time, Fedor P. - is Fyodor Panasevich. Juzef G., who helped her escape, was Juzef Golach and his friend was Vladimir Grigorevsky. Mrs. K. was Kozlovsky. Nicholai Zh, the man who hid Dora on the farmstead was Nicholai Zhuk. Mrs. K. was Keskevich. Mitya K. was Mitya Kozlowski. There was no name, not even the initials, of the policeman, who most likely was Leonid Nedeljko. Kozlovsky's girlfriend's name has not been determined, nor is the name of cousin Panasevich. Only once did Dora mention Volodya as Volodya, G. (Grigorevsky). Juzek G., the brother of Volodya, was Juzek Grigorevsky.

Dora called one village Zastavye, but it was not and does not exist. It is Zastavy, a suburb of Kamenets that is now incorporated into the town. All of the places where Dora hid were on Litewska Street (now Pivnenko Street) and on the farmstead in Uglyany. In her memoirs, Dora does not name any other places.

Old-timers say that Dora was very beautiful. Volodya (Vladimir), the son of the Kamenets butcher (sausage maker), Mikhas Grigorevsky, was fond of her. He received a good education and graduated from the "*techniczna*" (technical) school in Brest. When the Germans came, he was appointed the head of four mills, which were in Kamenets. Volodya lived on Senatorska Street [now 1st of May Street] and this also was a place where Dora hid some of the time.

When the Germans visited Volodya, they didn't know that behind the door covered with carpet was a Jew. It was a big risk and that is why Dora had to hide elsewhere. There is no doubt that Volodya organized her escape from the ghetto. He also arranged places for Dora to hide. He himself was put into a concentration camp in Pruzhany by the Germans for some fault in his job, but was released after a few weeks.

When Kamenets was freed from the Germans, Vladimir (Volodya) hid in the town from the Soviet regime, and then illegally moved to Poland. The underground relocated him and Juzef Golach to Poland. At that time, train drivers (motormen) smuggled people across the border for 10-ruble gold coins of tsarist Russia.

Ryszard Mankowski, a resident of the city of Lodz, said that Dora and Vladimir met in Poland and lived together, but for some reason they separated. Dora moved to Argentina and died there.

The rest of the cast of characters in Dora's memoirs are also dead.

The Removal of the Jewish Boys for Work

One day I went to a kiosk to buy a newspaper. While standing in line, I heard a conversation between a woman and the saleswoman. The woman repeated, "I don't understand, I don't understand." I realized that woman was Polish. I then said, "Say what you want madam and I will translate as best as I can." It turned out that the Polish woman wanted to buy postcards with current views of Kamenets. However, there were none. In conversation, she asked me whether I was from Kamenets. I responded in the affirmative. Then the Polish woman asked whether any of the Jews of Kamenets were alive. I replied that only Dora Galperin survived. The woman, who identified herself as Maria Brych, said that her husband Leon Gedalia Goldring, a Jew from Kamenets, survived the Holocaust. We exchanged addresses, and she asked me to find out about surviving Kamenets Jews and to report back to her.

In the summer of 1991, Leon and Maria knocked on my door. The man introduced himself in Polish: "*Jestem Leon Gedalia Goldring.* Please sir, I am able to speak Polish, Yiddish, and the Kamenets language." Wow! Almost 50 years passed since Leon was forced to leave his native land and the language of his people -- the north Volhynian dialect of the Ukrainian language -- where he lived harmoniously and he remembered.

He spent three days with me. I was his guide and drove him to Kamenets, which was a new town to him. He remembered the old streets, old quarters, and the Jewish homes where his friends who no longer exist lived. He remembered how, as a child, he played with the Salamonovicz children, who lived near his home. Leon asked me to find Janek Salamonovicz. We found him quite ill. Nevertheless, they recalled their trouble-free childhood. In parting, Leon gave Janek $100. Janek refused, but Leon insisted that he take it, as it would be useful for medications to treat him.

We walked around the town and he remembered and recalled. Speaking about his last days in Kamenets, Leon said, "The Germans herded us into ghettos. One day, they demanded that the *Judenrat* allocate 30 strong, young men to work. My name was drawn. I was only 17 years old. There on the edge of the former area of the market was a German vehicle, which was to take us to who knows where. But there," he pointed, "stood my dear mother with her head hung in grief. This was the last time I saw her." With these words, two large tears ran down Leon's cheeks. He continued on: "We 30 people were taken to repair the railway station in Volkovysk. After finishing the repairs, we ended up in the camp at Auschwitz (Oświęcim). When the camp was liberated, I was the only one left of the 30 people in the group. By the will of providence, I survived! But I lost all of my relatives. My mother, father, brother, and sister had been killed. I could not go back to Kamenets. I went to America and became a citizen. I worked as an assistant baker. I worked hard and made provisions for my old age. I have adult children. My wife died and I married a second time. But the memories of those years are depressing."

Closing of the Ghetto

In the area of the Kamenets District in 1941-1942 there were three ghettos, one in Volchin, the second in the Wysokie, and the third in Kamenets. The Volchin ghetto was destroyed in the fall of 1942. The Nazis dismantled the Wysokie ghetto in January 1942 and Kamenets in November 1942.

In the report on February 19, 1945 of the Commission of Inquiry of Nazi Atrocities in Kamenets, the following was noted: In the fall of 1942, of the Jewish population of 5,000 people living in Kamenets, only the elderly, women, and children remained. All of their valuables, clothing, and household implements were taken from them and they were expelled in the direction of Wysokie. Their fate is unknown.

Andrei Potoka, a Kamenets resident, said about the acts of Nazi atrocities in the Kamenets District, "In autumn 1942 the entire population of the ghetto was taken to the town of Wysokie where, after extensive torture and abuse, they were annihilated."

In his book, "A Memorial of the Genocide in the Territory of Brest Region," Marat Botvinnick wrote, "In the fall of 1942, the entire Jewish population of the town of Kamenets was taken to the Wysokie concentration camp, where they were killed after extensive torture and abuse." (p. 129).

Andrei Potoka and Marat Botvinnik were incorrect about the duration of time the Kamenets Jews spent in the Wysokie ghetto. In fact, they were there for several days. The Nazis killed many of them in Wysokie. Most of them were sent in freight cars from the Wysokie-Litovsk station to the death camp in Treblinka.

Here is what was told about the closing of the ghettos in Wysokie and Kamenets by witnesses Józef Charyton and Vasyl Troychuk.

Wysokie resident Charyton was an artist who devoted his work to Jewish themes – themes of Jewish life, culture, suffering, and death. Józef Charyton recalled: "In an early morning in late January 1942, the closing of the Wysokie ghetto began. The Nazis, to disguise their actions to eradicate all of the Jews in the ghetto, divided all of the Jews of the community into three parts. For the first part, they selected healthy men in the prime of their lives on the pretext of sending them to cut timber. Each carried a saw. As soon as the column was out of town, it was surrounded from nowhere by Nazi soldiers on foot and on horses. The walking was accelerated to jogging by savage blows from whips. The weaker and those weighed down with bags threw them to the ground and could not lift the bags."

Józef was really sorry that he had not seen the end of the running and decided to wait for the second stage at all costs. He went to the railway station again two days later.

Józef moved together with the column to the outskirts of the town. In open terrain, it was impossible to observe. He hid behind poplar trees and from there watched the column, while remaining unnoticed.

The third and final part of the Wysokie Jewish ghetto consisted of the elderly, the sick, women, girls, and children who were brought to the ghetto in carts like firewood. It was a horrible sight. Despite the demands and beatings to speed up, the convoy of carts stretched from Wysokie to the railway station. In the convoy of carts, the people cried and screamed. The Germans started to get nervous. A lot of people could have escaped, but no one did, because each was burdened with family ties and children. There were also those who were almost unconscious.

Józef went to the train station, stopping behind pillars. The scene of the loading into the box cars was horrible. The Jews were driven like cattle to the slaughterhouse, beaten and herded like horses. The unfortunate literally fell over each other in the freight cars, tearing their clothes, and losing shoes and hats. The loading lasted 7 to 10 minutes. The cars were locked tight and the locomotive pulled the train in a direction known to be to the death camp at Treblinka.

Józef intended to re-create history of the horrible, tragic scene on large canvasses. Unfortunately, the lack of material means (tools and equipment), relocating, and the lack of a permanent residence prevented him from executing his plan for a long time. Many of his works simply disappeared, but some were passed on to his friends, among them being a professor at the Jagellonian University (in Krakow, Poland), Dr. Jan Perdenya, and a priest named Wierobej, who was the priest in Hajnowka. Both of them were from Kamenets-Litovsk and Józef became acquainted with them there. Most of Józef's paintings are in the Jewish Historical Institute in Poland.

Vasyl Troychuk, a farmer from the village of Komarovshchina near Kamenets, witnessed the closing of the Kamenets ghetto. He had a cart in which he had to transport the unfortunate to Wysokie. "In the final elimination of the Kamenets ghetto, the Nazis moved all of the Jews in Kamenets to Wysokie at the beginning of November 1942. A large number of police, assistant-police, and *Sonderkommando* arrived. The area *Komissar* (commissar) ordered the residents of nearby villages to come to Kamenets at an appointed time. Horse-cab drivers were selected to harness a pair of horses to their carts and to put them in a column of six. The Nazis forced the Jewish men out of the ghetto to Market Square. The women, elderly, and the children put their belongings into the carts. The men were on foot and on the sides were guards. The route was from Kamenets to Zamosty to Voyskaya to Borshchevo to Muravchitsy to Dolbnyovo to Wysokie. Sometimes the sounds of gunshots were heard. The monsters were killing people who lagged behind (stragglers). Along the entire route (it was an offshoot of the old "Royal Way") the convoy was under the surveillance of the guards.

"Upon arriving in Wysokie, all were herded into the Wysokie ghetto that was empty by that time. The Nazis did not allow the Jews to take with them the things they brought with them and ordered them to leave them in the carts (wagons). The horse-cab drivers (cabbies) were ordered to drive to the railway station and to unload the items there.

"A few days later, they were put into freight cars. They were malnourished because of a lack of food during the days in Wysokie. The Nazis herded the Jews of Kamenets by foot in a column to the Wysokie-Litovsk train station and there herded them into the freight cars to take them to their death in Sobibor or maybe in Treblinka." (Recorded on 11/18/1997. The witness is dead.)

After the removal of the Jews from Kamenets, the barbed wire of the ghetto was removed. Some of the homes remained and some were given to Germans to move into. Dilapidated homes were sold for firewood. Displaced persons in need of housing settled in the remaining houses. These were deportees from the villages surrounding the Bialowieza Forest that the Germans evicted from their homes in August 1941 and burned the villages. Jewish assets remaining after the closing of the ghetto were given by the Germans to the local population. This does not mean that all local people received these assets, but, as always at all times and everywhere, to those few who were ready to commit and perform immoral acts. There were some groups of looters, who walked through the empty Jewish homes with drills and ramrods (crowbars) and drilled holes in the floors and felt under the floors to see if there was any buried jewelry. The Germans acted unconditionally and severely with the looters. I am aware of two cases in which the Germans shot and killed two looters on Kobrynska Street (now Chkalov Street). Apparently, this also happened in Wysokie after the elimination of the ghetto.

No Jews remained in the Kamenets area. Different people identify a different number of victims. According to my calculations, which are fairly accurate, the Germans killed 6,921 Jews and more than 1,500 people from among Soviet officials, activists, underground fighters, prisoners of war, and those who were not loyal to the German authorities. In total, the Nazis killed more than 8.5 thousand people, which was 17.3% of the population at that time.

Few individuals, two from Kamenets - Dora Galperin and Leon Gedalia Goldring - and one from Wysokie - Shloma Kantarovich, survived the hellish Holocaust. However, those who left Kamenets, Wysokie, and the agricultural colonies of Lotovo, Sarovo, and Abramovo before the war escaped the tragic fate of their fellow countrymen and remained alive. After the war, only Jewish newcomers lived in Kamenets. As far as I know, there was a teacher, Rachel Gordon, Tsodikov an officer at the District Military Recruitment Office, a barber, a musician from Riga named Weinstein, the director of the school, Valery Vodopyanov, Tsofina, the chairman of GORPO (Urban Consumer Society), and Boris Bedok, a shoemaker. All of them have since died. Weinstein had two daughters. One is a music teacher who lives in Germany; the second, a businesswoman who lives in Kamenets. Boris Bedok had a son and a daughter. The son is a music teacher and lives in Kamenyuki. The daughter is a homemaker (literally: *housewife*) and lives in Wysokie. Tsofina (after marriage Nicheporuk, have two daughters. One is a teacher who lives in Kamenets. The second is a teacher (lecturer) at the Institute of Foreign Languages and lives in Minsk.

In Kamenets Thirty Years Later

Dov (Berchik) Schmidt, the son of the owner of the meat shop that was at the beginning of Kobrynska Street (now Chkalova Street) had the first telephone in Kamenets-Litovsk. Before the World War II, he left for the United States for a better life. He left his bride, Elichka, in Kamenets. Being a decent man, sometime later he brought her to him. Then they moved to Israel. Dov remembered his native town and wanted to go there, but was able to only many years after the war. He wanted to see Dora Galperin, who was alive, having survived the Holocaust of the Jews. In Kamenets, he met up with Juzek Grigorewski, whom he had known since childhood.

For a long time there was a legend that the Israel Agriculture Minister, Beck, visited Juzek Grigorewski in Kamenets. Actually, it was Kamenets-born Dov (Berchik) Schmidt, an expert on fisheries. He described his experience in his travel notes published in a memorial book that is read throughout the Jewish world. We will use part of his notes to describe what he stated.

In 1965, Dov learned that he was allowed to participate in a seminar on fisheries that was scheduled in Moscow in the Soviet Union. His interest was not only in the seminar, but also in the possibility that he might visit the graves of his relatives and ancestors in his native Kamenets. Further, along the route, he was going to call on Dora Galperin to learn the details of the disaster in Kamenets. He knew that Dora lived in Poland. Of course, he knew that no graves of dead Kamenets Jews remained. Nevertheless, he wanted to see it all for himself. After obtaining a visa at the Soviet Union Embassy, Dov was allowed to go to Brest, and there he received permission to visit Kamenets.

In Brest, he explained to an employee of the Visa Office why he came from Israel to the Soviet Union. His purpose was simple - to pay a visit to his hometown. A pass to visit Kamenets was given to him, but on one condition, that being that the visit could not be for more than 5 hours.

In order to not waste precious time, Dov took a taxi for the journey to Kamenets. On this brief trip, Clara Satir, a native of Kamenets, Masha

Shcherba, a native of Brest, and a Jewish student from Bobruysk went with him.

Dov traveled the same road on which he traveled to Brest in his youth, but now it was wide and paved. He came to Chernavchitsy, where Jewish homes and what was Rachel Lykha's inn were still standing, but there were no Jews there. Next, near Vidomlya and Baranki, he saw train engine yards. At noon, the taxi arrived in Kamenets. Dov could hardly recognize the entrance to the town and Brzeska Street [now Brestskaya Street]. On the entire length of the street were new brick houses. Windmills were no longer there. Only Yosel Shostakovsky's windmill was still standing and it did not move during his visit. The windmills that once stood on historic Kladucha Hill had been destroyed. In place of the priest's house (the home of the Catholic priest), stood the three-storey building of the district's Executive Committee. In the area in front of the building stood a monument to Lenin. On the site of the houses was a general shopping center, similar to a supermarket. Dov wrote in his travel memoirs that the old Catholic church and town hall were gone. This was not entirely so. The old, wooden Catholic church burned down in 1924. After the fire it was rebuilt out of wood, but it was again destroyed by fire. In 1959, a brick building, which was begun before the war as a Catholic church, was completed. The Soviets made it into a cafeteria. In his memoirs, Dov called it a restaurant. After Belarus gained its independence, the Catholic community achieved the return of the building to a church that is built in a pre-war design. As for the town hall, it was called a *"magistrat"* and was located in the private home of a paramedic named Stasiak. The house is still standing. Near the church used to be a wooden bus station. A large brick bus station was built after 1965 on a plot of land called Busnyavka on Białostocka Street (now Pogranichnaya Street). Dov wrote that it was difficult to recall the images of the town that were imprinted in the memory of his youth. These were superficial images of his hometown. Its living spirit was not the same. However, once at Market Square, Dov recognized familiar places. Market Square also looked different. In place of the former Jewish shops there was a public park, in the center of which was a monument to the soldiers who died in World War II. According to Dov, houses were around the square as before as if nothing has changed. (From the author: Later the houses were gone and in their place a school was built.)

Dov wrote in his notes: "The houses of Galperin, Rabbi Vigutov, Rabbi Yitzchok, Shmul Golobchik, and David Rosenstock, and the Ossovsky pharmacy were not destroyed. The facades of the wooden houses on the surrounding streets and alleys to Kobrynska Street have not changed, but the porches have disappeared. Most of the streets are still paved with cobble stones. The sidewalks were old and decrepit." (From the author: Now, on the contrary, most of the streets are paved and the sidewalks are lined with tiles. Most of the houses have running water and many have natural gas. Beautiful brick houses line the southwest, south, and east sides.)

Dov wrote: "The synagogue "Der Meyer," together with the Talmud Torah school, was turned into a factory. The Kamenets Tower was renovated and houses the Museum of the Bialowieza Forest." (From the author: Dov was mistaken. This is not a Museum of the Bialowieza Forest, but it is a branch of the Brest Regional Museum.)

Dov continued to wander the old streets. He looked into the windows of the houses and tried to comprehend what he saw and to answer the question of why everything remained as it was, but life itself had disappeared. It seemed to him that the present people of the town just did not understand, or did not want to understand, what happened here.

Some people who met Dov on the street looked surprise upon learning that he was a Jew, who was a native of Kamenets. Upon learning this, the people reacted in different ways. Some were shocked and others recalled unpleasant memories.

Dov did not forget to visit the house of Juzek Grigorewsky. Juzek was touched more by the meeting than was Dov. Juzek kept repeating: "They were all killed. I was able to save only one and then only with great difficulty! None of you remained." Dov walked around the town with Juzek. People asked, "Who is this person?" Juzek said, "Don't you remember Chiam Schmidt's son?" When he passed the former Litewska Street with Juzek, an old Christian woman and her children came out of the yard of her house and asked, "Are you, by chance, the son of Chiam Schmidt, the butcher?" Receiving an affirmative reply, the woman burst into tears, and rushed to him and kissed him. The woman lamented: "How could those wild animals kill you! Why was your fate so bitter? Your father and mother and the whole family were good, decent people! Are there any Jews from Kamenets left in the world?" This honorable Christian grieved and wept with Dov.

Looking around the town of his childhood and adolescence, Dov could not help but go to the house where he was born and lived until age 19. Dov knocked on the door and walked into the premises. Toward the left, an old woman came out of the former bedroom of his parents. At first he could not say anything as tears choked him. The woman picked up on his state of mind and whispered, "Yes, I knew the owners of this house - Chiam, Rachel, their children, and grandchildren. They were good people and did good for others. The Nazis killed them! Oh, my God, is that our fault that the authorities then disposed of these households?" Dov could no longer stand it and went out into the yard with a broken heart. Children were playing there. They played happily, as he had once played. Seeing his camera, they asked him to photograph them. Dov photographed the children against the backdrop of his former home. It was the only picture he took to remember his native town.

An hour later, when he had calmed down, he decided to go to the District Executive Committee in hopes of getting at least some official information about the tragic death of the Jews in his hometown. With these thoughts, Dov Schmidt went into Executive Committee and told the clerk the purpose of his visit to Kamenets, and his great desire to learn the fate of the 500 Jewish families. Among them were his parents, sister, aunts, and uncles. The state official was frosty and coldly said, "Citizen! You can see everything that there is. We have no interest in what happened in the past. You are allowed to see everything that is around and come to your own conclusions. That's all." With these short, glib, and dry words, the representative of the authorities at once erased the past century's way of life of many generations of the small Jewish town.

When Dov left the Executive Committee, the five hours he was permitted had passed. Finding that his time in Kamenets had expired, Dov got into a taxi and, without turning around, said, "Let's go!" to the driver. He was out of breath and felt as if he was returning from a funeral – the funeral of his parents, sisters, uncles, aunts, friends, and acquaintances – Jews who once lived here in his home town of Kamenets. At the end of his travel notes, Dov emphasized to all that everyone should remember to tell the true story to their descendants!

Open Letter

In the late 1990s, I had the opportunity to be a member of the Coordinating Council for the Conservation of Historical and Cultural Heritage for some time. I did not want to and could not be a member of this Council in name only. Therefore, I sent an open letter to the Regional Executive Committee of Kamenets. The letter read:

Shortsightedness is our chronic disease. On one hand, the powers that be in this area suffer from myopia about the historical past and a real future. On the other hand, we all (with rare exceptions) are indifferent to the suffering of others. Are our memories as short-lived as the life of a moth?

Despite the fact that the pages of our only regional newspaper have repeatedly written about the destruction of tombstones monuments in the old Christian cemetery, the tombstones of the Jewish cemetery were used as steps. There was an unlawful destruction of the *dom ludowy* (people's house; i.e., building built in the Polish period and used for public functions) and the old *Zemstvo* Hospital. No one lifted a finger, no one responded verbally to this treatment, and no one responded to statements in the newspaper. Surprisingly, all of this was happening right before our eyes, not somewhere in the outskirts, but rather in the center of the District capital. I'm not mentioning the other objects that could be rescued.

All the same, in life we are forced to turn to our historical past. As a result, in late 1996, the Coordinating Council for the Conservation of Historical and Cultural Heritage was formed. The organization was timely and necessary. A year has passed since its inception, and I have some concerns that the Council was left without counsel. God grant it was otherwise.

At 8 Podrzeczna Street (now Naberezhnaya Street), opposite the present day military enlistment office, there was a large brick building built in the late 19th and early 20th centuries. Most Kamenets residents now call this Consumer Services (Bytkombinat). After the war, it was a molasses factory, and a "Raduga" and a "Troika" shop. It is now owned by a farmer. This building was originally a large synagogue, "Der Meyer."

In the center of the synagogue were four cast-iron columns. On the walls were plants and frescoes. Now there are none. The columns remain. As a result of numerous repairs and modifications, little remains of the original architectural appearance of the synagogue. After completing regular repairs, the columns will not be visible, because the new owner does not want them visible. Builders argue that no damage would be done if the wall of the oval was made deeper. The columns would then be visible in the corridor.

As a member of the Coordinating Council and as a citizen of this town, I submit the inquiry to the municipal and regional authorities:

1. Who sold the building, this architectural landmark, whether there was a contract for the conservation of at least parts of the architectural appearance of the building to be intact, and whether requirements to preserve it were secured?
2. Was the Coordinating Council notified of the sale of the building that is an architectural landmark?
3. Will the people responsible for the sale or rent of similar cultural or historical monuments coordinate the sale or rent of similar buildings with the Coordinating Council?
4. Pending the sale or lease of buildings belonging to architectural or historic monuments, will the new owner or lessee have to meet preservation requirements?

The issues raised relate not only to a single fact, but to cultural and historical heritage. (Georgiy Musevich, "Kamyanechchyny News" January 14 - 15 1998)

The answer I received, signed by deputy chairman of the Executive

Committee, N. Woytsik, was a standard official reply in which there is no hint of a change in the situation.

The Ashes of the Homes and the People

Kamenets-Litovsk is no longer inhabited by Jews. There are no Jews, no Jewish culture or way of life. They were killed and burned in the crematoria ovens. Kamenets is completely different. The descendants of those Jews who left Kamenets before the war to different countries were born far away in other countries and travel to Kamenets. It is difficult to say how many of them have come to Kamenets and Wysokie. I can only name those who have communicated with me as a local historian and, in part, as a witness of the past. Their names are:

1. Ziefert Kieffer - grandson of Rabbi David Stempnitsky with his wife - United States, Ann Arbor, (Michigan) 1994
2. Leon Gedalia Goldring and his wife - United States, 1991
3. Krawczyk - the United States, 1998
4. Alex Kessler, the Cultural Center of Israel - Minsk, 1999
5. Kozhi Khan - United States, 1999
6. Miguel Kaplansky and his wife - Argentina, Buenos Aires, 2001
7. Rabbi Mordukhai Rayhinshteyn - Kiev, 2001
8. Dubrovski - Minsk, 2003
9. Howard Hirsch - United States, Livingston, New Jersey 2005
10. Gloria Hirsch – United States, Livingston, New Jersey 2005
11. Dr. Arthur Friedman - United States, Washington, DC 2005
12. Shana Egan – United States, San Diego, California 2005
13. Rabbi (last name unknown) - Israel, 2006
14. Flusberg, grandson of Sarah Morgenstern - United States, 2006
15. Akiva Bergman - Israel, 2007
16. Chief Rabbi of Brest, Chiam Rabinowitz – 2008
17. Rabbi (last name unknown) - Israel, 2008
18. Henry Neugass - United States, 2007

The question is: Why do they come, what is it that they need, and what are they looking for? They come to see the town of their ancestors, or where they themselves were born, to wander through the old streets, to find the homes of their parents, to worship at the graves in the cemeteries, to see the House of Prayer, to go to the river near which previous generations lived, and to breathe the air that was breathed by their fathers, mothers, grandparents, and their close and distant relatives. They want to learn about the tragedy that occurred in Kamenets. They can see everything that they want to see and they can breathe the native air, but they cannot worship at the graves as the cemeteries have been destroyed. They cannot see all the houses of prayer, except one that was converted into housing and a second that was converted into the House of Culture. The witnesses of the tragedy in Kamenets are almost gone.

Jews who come are very pleased when they can see the homes of their parents and grandparents. With my help, we managed to find Miguel Kaplansky's father's house; the house of David Stempnitsky, Kieffer's grandfather; the place where the house of Gloria Hirsch's grandfather, Cantor Hesker Yaffe, stood; the place where the soda water (sparkling water) factory of Sarah Morgenstern's grandmother, Flusberg, stood.

Jews who come to the town of their ancestors are not able to see a monument to victims of the Holocaust, because it does not exist. I ask myself, why are there no monuments or memorial signs in places where the Nazis executed the Jews on the Rovets tract of land, at Peshchany, in the Vorohovsky Forest near the village of Malaya (Small) Turna. I cannot find an answer. I cannot say that there have not been steps taken to establish a monument in Kamenets. There have been, but to no avail. The monument to the Jewish victims of fascism would be put in Wysokie.

Miguel Kaplansky of Buenos Aires commissioned a translator from Brest, Eugene Poleshchuk, to determine whether it was possible for Kaplansky to erect a monument to the victims of the Holocaust in Kamenets and a memorial sign on the Rovets tract of land. Poleshchuk and I visited the Vice-President of the District Executive Committee, Nikolai Woytsik. He gave consent subject to certain requirements. The District Architect had to agree to where the monument and memorial sign were to be placed. However, there was no answer to a letter sent to Miguel Kaplansky. He was an older man and died without receiving an answer.

In September 2005, Brest was visited by 34 representatives of the international genealogical research group, "Briskers." This genealogy organization examines the history of the Jews of Brest. "Brisk" is the Jewish name of Brest, hence the word "Brisker," a resident of Brest. In general, it has about 200 members from the United States, Canada, and the United Kingdom. In addition, there are members from Russia, Belarus, Australia, South Africa, New Zealand, Brazil, and Argentina. These are the descendants of those Jews who once lived in the land of the Brest region, including Kamenets-Litovsk. One of the purposes for the visitors coming was the unveiling of a plaque honoring Nobel Prize winner, Menachem Begin, the Prime Minister of the State of Israel, who was born in Brest, in a memorial park that was created and funded with the help of city officials, and is located next to where the Brest Jewish cemetery was located.

Members of the group, Howard Hirsch and his wife, Gloria, whose ancestors came from Kamenets, visited the town and for two days they walked through places memorable to them. Howard and Gloria paid a visit to the Deputy Chairman of the District Executive Committee, Nikolai Woytsik, presented him with a commemorative book on the history of the Jews of Kamenets, and expressed the wish to establish a monument at their expense to the Kamenets Jews who perished in the flames of the Holocaust. Of all the places in Kamenets, they chose the eastern part of the park in the center of the town, citing the fact that the park is located on the site of the former Jewish shops that were demolished in 1940 near the synagogue, "Der Meyer," the spiritual center Jewish Kamenets, and near the *Judenrat* through which the Nazis sent hundreds of Jews to the Holocaust. Nikolai Woytsik responded positively to the proposal to erect a monument. Howard and Gloria Hirsch asked me to represent their organization's interests in this matter. So, in October of that year, I was back with Nikolai Woytsik, regarding the establishment of the monument. He said that Executive Committee did not see any obstacles, and referred me to the District Architect. I wrote an official letter to the Architect, Victoria Yarotsevich, who had agreed in principle and outlined the conditions for the establishment of the monument. I sent the terms and conditions to a third party in Minsk that was to be engaged in the technical aspects of the project. However, I have not received a response from them.

The case has stalled for some time. Nevertheless, we hope that memorials to the Holocaust victims from Kamenets and Wysokie and commemorative signs will be installed at the Rovets tract of land, at Peshchany, and in the Vorohovsky Forest near the village of Malaya (Small) Turna. This must be done before the witnesses go to a better world and memories of the events are lost.

Summer Flowers For The Doctor

Before the war, Kamenets was mainly a Jewish "shtetl" (town). More than four thousand Jews lived and worked there. They were engaged in various types businesses. Jews were masters of tailoring, footwear manufacture, and making confectionary products (pastry). They sold meat products, different types of flour, and agricultural implements. They were fantastic merchants, and buyers of cattle and raw materials from the peasants of the district. They even rented land and grew good harvests of vegetables and grains.

Dr. Golberg was famous throughout the Jewish community of Kamenets and the neighboring areas. He was a private physician, who lived in his own house at 13 Bialostocka Street (now Pogranichnaya Street) in Kamenets-Litovsk. The doctor had a family: his wife, daughter, Janeczka, son-in-law, Ludwig, and his son Hirsch. The house housed a 4 to 5 bed hospital. Dr. Golberg successfully treated people that were often considered hopeless, because they could not be treated by the doctors at the government (public) hospital, which was on Kobrynska Street (now Chkalova Street). Dr. Bogucki worked in this hospital for a long time. After examining a patient who was brought to him, the doctor often advised him to contact Golberg as the last hope of being saved. The conclusions of Dr. Golberg were definitive. He did not make mistakes regarding diagnoses. He was the doctor from God! In his treatment, he not only used medicines, but also herbal teas and massage. Of course, the patients paid for treatment, but the money did not compare to the return of health! Those who live today and were once patients of Golberg say there are very few doctors like him now.

Early in the spring of 1936, a peasant family brought their young son, who was less than a year old, for treatment at the public hospital. The sick child was examined by Doctor Bogucki who openly said that he was not sure that the boy would live, because the illness had progressed too far and the cost would be considerable. Every day of the child's stay in the hospital would cost 5 zlotys (PLN). He advised the family to contact Dr. Golberg. With tears in their eyes, and with sad thoughts, the peasants drove their child to Golberg. After examining the child, he confirmed that the baby was on the verge of death. Treatment would cost 25 zlotys (PLN).

"Do you have that kind of money?" asked the doctor. The father of baby remarked that he had just 5 zlotys in his pocket (this was the price of 50 kg. of grain). "I'll go to a Jewish friend and borrow the money" he promised, in the hope that the boy will be saved, and he rushed to the door.

The doctor was not listening as he bustled around the child. When the man returned with the money, the doctor said to him, "Go home and let your wife stay with the baby. Do not worry, your son will live." And indeed, after a week, the peasant went to town to pick up his wife and son. The boy was very well, peppy, and sputtered something in a child's language. It only remains to add that the peasants were my father, Nicholai Stepanovich, and my mother, Maria Mikhailovna. The boy was my brother Ivan, who for the past 42 years has been a Doctor after graduating from the Belarusian State Medical University in Minsk and now works as a physician at a plant where prosthetics are manufactured, Ivan Nikolayevich Mamus.

Dr. Golberg's whole family died in the spring of 1942 on the edge of the forest near Dmitrovichi by the hands of the Nazi occupiers. Their only fault was that they were Jews. The Germans systematically destroyed the Jewish nation without pity. A platoon of police led by a local Fascist henchman named Garah, who was originally from Osinniki, delivered the family to the police station from a shed on a farm near Smuga. When the Germans retreated from Kamenets, Garah fled with them to Poland. After the war, he was found and punished as a criminal.

When my brother and his family visit me, we always go to the place where his savior, Dr. Golberg, and his family are buried. Ivan lays flowers on the grave and kneels and bows his head before the mighty Doctor and his wife and two sons.

In Kamenets, the former Golberg home is painted in a light white color. Two families are living there. Life goes on. (Michael Mamus, teacher, "Kamyanechchyny News" 02/18/1998).

Background

The Area Population of Jews in 1939

1. Kamenets-Litovsk	3,909 (92.1% of the residents of Kamenets-Litovsk)
2. Wysokie-Litovsk	2,000
3. Volchin	402
4. Abramovo	172
5. Verhovichi	79
6. Sarovo	56
7. Lotovo	48
8. Tokari	36
9. Ryasno	36
10. Dmitrovichi	28
11. Pashuk	25
12. Velikiy Lyes (Great Forest)	23
13. Rechitsa	23
14. Lishnya	15
15. Voyskaya	14
16. Puzhitsy	11
17. Bolshaya (Big) Turna	10
18. Trostyanitsa	9
19. Vidomlya	8
20. Omelenets	7
21. Gorodyshche	3
22. Radost	3
23. Baranki	3
24. Leshanka	1

Total: 6,921 people - 16% of the total population of the district.

Occupations of the Residents of Kamenets-Litovsk

	Christians	Jews	Total
1. Painters		5	5
2. Glaziers		3	3
3. Turners		2	2
4. Wheelwrights	1	3	4
5. Harness Cart Drivers ("Balagoly")		17	17
6. Blacksmiths	1	7	8
7. Watchmakers		3	3
8. Harness Makers		5	5
9. Tanners		6	6
10. Slaughters/Ritual Slaughters ("Schochets")		12	12
11. Photographers		2	2
12. Concrete Workers	1	3	4
13. Cabinet Makers / Wood Workers	5	7	12
14. Carpenters	2	3	5
15. Hat and Cap Makers		5	5
16. Tailors	2	13	15
17. Tinsmiths	1	1	2
18. Locksmiths	1	2	3
19. Beggars ("Schnorers")		7	7
20. Shoemakers / Cobblers	4	48	52
21. Bakers	1	9	10
22. Butchers	3	2	5
23. Hairdressers		4	4
24. Millers	4	7	11
25. Porters		2	2
26. Teachers	8	16	24
27. Librarians	1	3	4
28. Pharmacists	1	2	3
29. Paramedics	2	2	4
30. Doctors	1	3	4
31. Attorneys		1	1

32. Veterinarians	1		1
33. Electricians	1	2	3
34. Mechanics	4	0	4
35. Government Officials	11	1	12
36. Clergymen	2	28	30
37. Nurses	4	2	6
38. Agriculture / Farmers	149	2	151
39. Wool Spinners	1	2	3
40. Coffee House/Tea Room/Café Workers		1	1
41. Brickmakers		2	2
42. Rag Pickers		2	2
43. Bicycle Servicing		1	1
44. Handymen	15	95	110
45. Merchants, Shopkeepers	6	192	198
46. Drivers	1	1	2
47. Female Bakery Workers		9	9
48. Creamery Workers		3	3
Total	234	548	782

We must bear in mind that the masters had apprentices and students that are not listed here.

The Number of Jewish and Christian Houses in Kamenets-Litovsk

Name of Streets and Squares	Jews			Christians			Together
	Wood	Brick	Total	Wood	Brick	Total	
1. Bzeska	61	4	65	3	0	3	68
2. Kobrynska	33	0	33	2	1	3	36
3. Litewska	15	1	16	38	0	38	54
4. Rynek (Market)	33	6	39	0	1	1	40
5. Dolina	4	0	4	2	0	2	6
6. Smocza	10	0	10	0	0	0	10
7. Mala	5	0	5	0	0	0	5
8 Krótka	2	0	2	0	0	0	2
9. Wąska	16	0	16	0	0	0	16
10. Scianka	0	0	0	1	0	1	1
11. Białostocka	29	0	29	18	0	18	47
12. Senatorska	2	0	2	45	0	45	47
13. Szkolna	11	0	11	0	0	0	11
14. Kościelna	0	0	0	3	0	3	3
15. Pasieka	0	0	0	3	0	3	3
16. Podrzeczna	14	7	21	1	0	1	22
17. Cmentarna	0	0	0	0	0	0	0
18. Polna	3	0	3	12	0	12	15
19. Peretsa	8	2	10	0	1	1	11
20. Bożnicza	2	11	13	0	0	0	13
21. Mościckiego	3	0	3	2	0	2	5
22. Pochyla	2	2	4	0	0	0	4
23. Zamkowa	18	0	10	0	0	0	18
24. Dojazd	7	2	9	1	0	1	10
25. Pszesmyk	7	2	9	1	0	1	10
26. Asza	11	2	13	0	0	0	13
27. Białowieska	0	0	0	1	0	1	1
28. Głęboka	6	0	6	2	0	2	8

29. Ogrodowa	7	0	7	0	0	0	7
30. Gminna	0	0	0	2	0	2	2
31. Kreta	4	0	4	2	0	2	6
32. Krzywa	3	0	3	0	0	0	3
33. Novo Senatorska	2	0	2	3	0	3	5
34. Przejazd Nadrzeczny	2	2	4	1	0	1	5
35. Murinka	0	0	0	4	0	4	4
36. Sądowa	0	0	0	8	0	8	8
37. Zajazd Kąpielowy	6	0	6	0	0	0	6
38. Szosowa	5	0	5	0	0	0	5
39. Plac Piłsudskiego	5	3	8	6	0	6	14
40. Targowa	3	0	3	0	0	0	3
Total	336	42	378	160	3	163	541

Street Names in Kamenets

During the time that Kamenets was part of Poland (1919-1939), the streets had Polish names. They were renamed by the Soviet authorities in 1939.

In addition to the streets in Kamenets-Litovsk before 1939, there were squares.

1. Pilsudski Square, near the current printing house.
2. A square without a name, near the current high school.
3. Church Square that is now the market place.
4. Rynek Square where there now is a mini-park and a mass grave of soldiers who died in the last war (WWII).

Polish Names	New Names (in capital letters)
1. Asza Street	From Brzeska Street to the Rynek (market). BRESTSKAYA
2. Bożnicza Street	From Litewska to Podrzeczna to the right of the "Der Meyer" Synagogue. This street does not exist today.
3. Białostocka Street	POGRANICHNAYA
4. Brzeska Street	BRESTSKAYA
5. Białowieska Street	From Ogrodowa to the gas turbine mill. Does not exist today.
6. Cmentarna Street	Bzheska to the old cemetery. Does not exist today..
7. Dojazd Street	From Bialostotska to the river. POGRANICHNAYA
8. Dolina Street	From Brzeska to Kobrynska. PROLYTARSKYA
9. Gleboka Street	From the Ossovsky house to Brzeska. Does not exist today.
10. Gminna Street	From Dojazd to Shkolna. Does not exist today.
11. Kobryńska Street	From the market on Rechytsa. CHKALOVA
12. Kościelna Street	From Brzeska to Senatorska. SOVIET
13. Kreta Street	From Dojazd to Szkolna. Does not exist today.
14. Krutka Street	From Kobrynska to Wąska. Does not exist today.
15. Krzywa Street	From Asha to Brzeska. Does not exist today.

16. Mala Street	From Kobrynska to Litewska. Does not exist today.
17. Novo Senatorska Street	From Senatorska to the Satsevichey House. Does not exist today.
18. Ogrodowa Street	Białostocka up to the bridges. POGRANICHNAYA
19. Mościckiego Street	From Podrzeczna to the corner of Białostocka. NABEREZNAYA
20. Pasieka Street	From Brzeska to Senatorska. LEVANEVSKOGO
21. Polna Street	From Dojazd to Brzeska. GOGOLYA
22. Pereca Street	From Litewska to Białostocka. Does not exist today.
23. Pochyla Street	From Podrzeczna to Pereca to the left of the Tower (i.e., Vezha). Does not exist today.
24. plac Piłsudskiego	Today's mini-park by the editor's / editorial office of the newspaper "Kamyanechchyny News".
25. Podrzeczna Street	From Litewska to Mościckiego. NABEREZNAYA (Embankment)
26. Przejazd Nadrzeczny Street	From Podrzeczna to the river and the current military enlistment office. NABEREZNAYA
27. Przesmyk Street	From Polna Street to Pereca. LENINA
28. Rynek (Market) Street	From Przesmyk to Białostocka. LENINA
29. Szkolna Street	From Białostocka to Podrzeczna down to the river. LENINA
30. Sadowa Street	From Kościelna southwards to the Court house. 40 LET (Years of the) BSSR (Byelorussian Soviet Socialist Republic)
31. Senatorska Street, Pocztowa Street	From Białostocka to Pasieka. 1-ogo MAYA (1st of MAY)
32. Szosowa Street	From Brzeska towards Zhabinka. 8-ogo MARTA (8th of MARCH)
33. Targowa Street	Brzeska to the left of the Agro-Industrial Bank to the Bazaar
34. Wąska Street	From Dojazd to Smocza and the former lemonade factory. SREDNYAYA
35. Zamkowa Street	From Pereca to the right of the Tower (i.e., Vezha) to Podrzeczna. Does not exist today.

36. Zajazd Kąpielowy Street	From Podrzeczna past the house of A. Prokopovich to the river. NABEREZNAYA
37. Ścianka Street	From Litewska to Goly Borok. Does not exist today.
38. Murinka Street	From the old Jewish cemetery "Kvores" to Bolshye (Big) Muriny. Does not exist today.
39. Smocza Street	From Kobrynska to Litewska. Does not exist today.
40. Litewska Street, Berko Joselewicza Street, Piłsudskiego Street	From Pereca to Uglany. PIVNENKO

Sixteen streets did not survive. They were absorbed by other streets or renamed. The essence of the historical street names are lost as is the historic character of the ancient town of Kamenets. Take, for example, Litewska Street. It passed through the centuries-old main highways: "The Royal," "Burshtynovy," and "Zvarnitsky." Or, for instance, Zamkowa Street. Its name says that once there was a castle in Kamenets. However, there is no trace of it now!

Epilogue

There are no longer Jews and perhaps their descendants there. And time marches on...but something remains. The spirits and shadows of synagogues are still wandering along narrow streets of our town. New buildings have appeared in Kamenets and Wysokie, but the atmosphere of those years has not been completely lost yet. There still are plain houses with shutters. Life in them continues. Some of them are separated from each other with firewalls. Their dates of construction that are noted are 1779, 1880, 1895, 1900, etc.

Still, though very rarely, you can see rusted keys from small storerooms. There still are places where once there were cemeteries, but they are now destroyed. Occasionally, discolored photographs of forgotten dark-haired girls are found and revive the memory of life before the war, but the memories are fewer and fewer. What else can I say?

In this world we find light and darkness, black and white, and good and evil. Some people are good and others bad. But how can an entire nation of people be considered bad? God created people in his own image. There is one God, but belief in him is different. Should people be despised and destroyed only on the basis that they have different blood, a different faith? The answer is unequivocally NO! And once again NO!

Somewhere in the twilight, the dark clouds have already gathered - harbingers of the storm. Old people often have a premonition about a change in weather, a storm.

In 1938, Vasyl from Komarovshchiny was sitting on a bench and speaking with an old Jew. The old Jew had a premonition of something terrible. The old Jew said, "Vasyl, there will be trouble for us. We are already in the bag. All that is left is to tie us up in it."

Anxiety gradually increased and in 1941 the terrible word "War!" sounded like thunder. The premonition of the old Jew had come true. A dark invasion came near to each home. First casualties. Soon the Nazis treated the Jews like animals and confined them to a ghetto behind barbed wire. Then they brought them to the crematoria ovens. There were a few, though, that tried to hide from the Nazis, but in most cases it was to no avail.

Leahs, Elichkas, Sarahs, Simchas, Rachels, Abrahams, Chiams, Yoselis, Boruchs, Pesachs, Moshes..... It is difficult to believe that very few people heard about the ghettos in Kamenets and Wysokie, about the barbed wire, about the executions, about the complete destruction and burning in the furnaces of the crematoria, and of the Holocaust committed by the Nazis.

Years have passed, the authorities have changed, and the silence around this remains. The memorials have not been put up in Kamenets[4] and Wysokie, and not on the Rovets tract of land, at Peshchany, in the Vorohovsky Forest, or near Malaya (Small) Turna.

After the Jews were taken to Wysokie, Kamenets suddenly became empty. The whole country was empty. Everything had ended. That old culture was gone from this world and would never return to this part of the world, to the forests in the vicinity of Kamenets: Murinsky, Prusskovsky, and Chemerskoy and in the vicinity of Wysokie - Penyechka and Borok, and to old, forgotten cemeteries. What were people looking for by breaking gravestones? Why did they disturb the souls of dead Jews? And if they found something, many have lost! They pulled out by force what belongs to eternity. The remaining tombstones paved roads, and were made into steps to walk down, and into grinding stones. Nothing is left of the cemeteries.

Sixty-six years have already passed since those tragic events of the Holocaust in Kamenets. We go further and further away into the distance from those sad events of the past. The grass grows higher and higher, the stones are covered with moss and all settle deeper and deeper into the ground. Only the shadows of the dead wander somewhere! May this book help new generations learn that among us lived such a people - the Jews.

Georgiy Musevich
2001-2008 year.
Kamenets – "Belaya Vezha" (White Tower) Health Spa – Kamenets

Sources

1. "Belarusian Past" № 3, 1994.
   Беларуская мінуўшчына №3, 1994
2. Oleg Anatol'evich Trusov *"Staronki muravanay knigi"* (Pages of the Stone Book; Monumental Architecture in the Age of Feudalism and Capitalism), Minsk, 1990.
   Алег Трусау «Старонкі мураванай кнігі» Мінск, 1990.
3. Lev Gumilev "Ancient Russia and the Great Steppe," p.74-75.
   Лев Гумилев «Древняя Русь и Великая степь» с.74-75.
4. "Our Life" - annual subscription for 1926.
   «Наше життя» - годовая подписка за 1926 год.
5. Josephus Flavius "Jewish Wars," Minsk, 1994.
   Иосиф Флавий «Иудейские войны» Минск, 1994.
6. Georgiy Musevich "My City" Kamenets, 1996.
   Георгий Мусевич «Мой город» Каменец, 1996.
7. "Kamyanechchyny News" № 75. Kamenets, 04/10/1995.
   "Навіны Камянеччыны" №75. Каменец, 4.10.1995.
8. Jan Perdenia *"Z dziejów gminy żydowskiej w Kamiencu-Litewskim"* (History of the Jewish Community in Kamenets-Litovsk), Kraków.
9. A.P.Ignatenko, V.N.Sidortsov "Reader on History of Belarus" p.p. 186,187, 232.
   А.П.Игнатенко, В.Н.Сидорцов «Хрестоматия по истории Белоруссии" с.с. 186,187,232.
10. Jenni Buch (Australia) Study Materials of the Kamenets Yeshiva, 2008.
11. Henry Neugass (USA) Research Materials of a Study of the Kamenets Yeshiva, 2008.
12. Roman Levin, "The Boy from the Ghetto" Moscow, 1996.
    Роман Левин "Мальчик из гетто" Москва, 1996 г.
13. Michal Mincewicz *"Żydzi w Orli,"* (Jews in Orla) "Czasopis" № 12, Białystok, 2007.
14. Józef Charyton *"Wysokie-Litewskie podczas okupacji hitlerowskiej"* (Wysokie-Litovsk During the Nazi Occupation), Nurzec, 1963.
15. Marat Botvinnik "Monuments of the Genocide in Brest Region," Minsk.
    Марат Ботвинник "Памятники геноцида на территории Брестчины" Минск.
16. Eugene Rosenblatt "Final Solution of the Jewish Question in the Western Regions of Belarus. 1941-1944," Minsk, 2000, p.129.
    Евгений Розенблат "Окончательное решение еврейского вопроса в Западных областях Беларуси. 1941-1944" Минск, 2000, с.129.

17. Semen Byokner "On the Resistance in the Bialystok Ghetto," Voronezh, 2000.
    Семен Бёркнер "О сопротивлении в Белостокском гетто" Воронеж, 2000.
18. Georgiy Musevich "Kamenets Magdeburg," "Kamyanechchyny News," Kamenets, 2,9, 16.09.1998.
    Георгий Мусевич "Каменецкая Магдебургия", " Навіны Камянеччыны", Каменец, 2, 9, 16.09.1998.
19. "Acts of Atrocities by the Nazis in the Kamenets District," 17,03,1945.
    "Акт злодеяний немецко-фашистских захватчиков в Каменецком р-не", 17.03.1945 г.
20. "Pamyats.Kamyanetski RANS" (Memory. Kamenets District) Minsk, 1997, p.205.
    "Памяць.Камянецкі раён" Мінск, 1997, с.205.
21. GABO (State Archives of the Brest Region) FA-2059, op. - 1; q-2956b, 1937-1938.
    ГАБО (Государственный архив Брестской области) ф.-2059, оп.- 1; д,-2956б, 1937-1938.
22. GABO FA-2059, op. - 1, d-2956a, 1932-1935.
    ГАБО ф.-2059; оп. - 1; д. -2956a, 1932-1935.
23. GABO FA-310; op.-1, etc. - 18, F-59, op.-2 d-700 License for the opening of Wysokie-Litovsk Jewish school.
    ГАБО Ф.-310; оп.-1; д.- 18, Ф-59, оп.-2, д.-700 Лицензия на открытие Высоко-Литовской еврейской школы.
24. GABO f.-59, op.-2, d.-683 - *Sprawozdanie rabinaskich szkół* (Report of the Rabbinical Schools), 1938.
25. GABO f.-2001, op.- 4, d.-2745.
    ГАБО ф.-2001, оп.- 4, д.- 2745.
26. GABO f.-1, op-0, d.-25-85.
    ГАБО ф.-1, оп.-10, д.- 25-85.
27. GABO f.-28, op.-8, d.-16-64.
    ГАБО ф.-28, оп.-8, д.-16-64.
28. GABO - 1931, p. 1133, 1937, 11 346, 1938, p. 10 187, 1939, 11 347, "Rocznik ziem wschodnich" (Yearbook of the Eastern Regions).
29. "The Act of the Crimes the Nazis in the Belianskaya Village Council." 1944.
    "Акт о преступлениях фашистов в Белянском сельском совете". 1944.
30. GABO f.–r514, op.-1, d-41, p.-17.
    ГАБО ф. р-514, оп.-1, д.-41, л.-17.
31. GABO f.-59; op.-2, d.-683.
    ГАБО ф.-59; оп.-2; д.-683.

32. Mihail Mamus "Summer Flowers For The Doctor" – "Kamyanechchyny News" Kamenets, 02,18,1998.
    Михаил Мамус "Цветы лета - Доктору"- "Навіны Камянеччыны"Каменец, 18.02,1998.
33. Memories of Eyewitnesses: Pavell Gorbatsevich, Vasyl Troychuk, Anna Budko, Michael Korolyuk, Leo Sachko, Eugene Keskevich, Leon Gedalia Goldring, Zinaida Krechko, Vasyl Demenchuk, Gary Kardychkin, Nicholai Romaniuk, Georgiy Musevich, Stephen Musevich, Ryszard Mankowski, Yuri Saharchuk, Anna Musevich, Andrey Kharkov, Gregory Zaretsy, Jaroslav Mushits, Shleyme Kantarovich, Vladimir I. Grigorevsky, Vladimir Zhitinets, Andrei Potoka, Jakov Potoka, Adelina Grushevskaya, Ada Jakubowska, V.Brishchuk, P.Zhuk, V.Pilipchuk.
    Воспоминания очевидцев: Павел Горбацевич, Васыль Тройчук, Анна Будько, Михаил Королюк, Лев Сачко, Евгений Кескевич, Леон Гедалье Гольдринг, Зинаида Кречко, Васыль Деменчук, Гарий Кардычкин, Николай Романюк, Георгий Мусевич, Стефан Мусевич, Рышард Маньковски, Юрий Сахарчук, Анна Мусевич, Андрей Харько, Зарецкий Григорий, Ярослав Мушиц, Кантарович Шлема, Владимир Иванович Григоревский, Владимир Житинец, Андрей Потока, Яков Потока, Аделина Грушевская, Ада Якубовска, В.Брищук, П.Жук, В.Пилипчук.
34. "Słownik geograficzny Królestwa Polskiego i innych krajów słowiańskich" (Geographical Dictionary of the Polish Kingdom and Other Slavic Countries), Warszawa (Warsaw), 1895.
35. Memorial book of Kamenets Litovsk, Zastavye and colonies. (Memorial Book), Tel-Aviv, 1967.
36. Hatzkel Kagan "The Years of my Youth in Kamenets-Litovsk" (Memorial Book).
37. Itzhak Sheinfeld "Kamenets - The Memories of My Youth" (Memorial Book).
38. Charles Raddock "The Kamenetzer Yeshiva of America" (Memorial Book).
39. Leybl Golberg "The Beginning of Jewish Settlement in Kamenets" (Memorial Book).
40. Abraham Shudroff "Yearning and Mourning for My Home Town" (Memorial Book).
41. Dov (Berchik) Schmidt "My Journey to Kamenets in 1965" (Memorial Book).
42. Velvel Kustin "The Jewish Agricultural Colonies" (Memorial Book).
43. Yehezkel Kotik "My Reminiscences" (Memorial Book).
44. Dora Galperin "The Tragedy and Destruction of Kamenets" (The Letters of Dora to Lea and Dov Aloni) (Memorial Book).

45. Berel Wein, "Triumph of the Salvation Story of the Jews of Modern History 1650-1990."
46. Ruchoma Shain "All for the Boss: The Life and Impact of R'Yaakov Yosef Herman, a Torah Pioneer in America: An Affectionate Family Chronicle," 2001.
47. Janusz Korbel Reviews and presentations. "*Czasopis.*" № 5, Białystok, 2008.
48. Janusz Korbel "Człowiek i las," (Man and the Forest), Białowieża, 2005.
49. Oleg Medvedevsky - consulting, translation, editing, and preparation of the book to be published.
50. Original Cover design, http://www.kamenets.by/

Notes

Page 14
[1] The formation of Jewish agricultural colonies in the Russian Empire was dated as "around the beginning of the eighteenth century," whereas they were started at the beginning of the nineteen century as a result of a famine in the late 1700s, according to the Jewish Encyclopedia and others. The three colonies were established around 1850.
http://www.jewishencyclopedia.com/articles/908-agricultural-colonies-in-russia

Page 44
[2] Nemtsovich was the last town owner before WWI broke out. The government bought back the rights to sell vodka to restrict or eliminate vodka sales in Russia in the early 20th century. This attempt at was similar to the attempt by the United States government to eliminate alcoholic drinks in the 1930s through prohibition and also was a failure.

Page 80
[3] Some of the people mentioned in this paragraph settled the colony of Sarovo in about 1850. The date referred to here regarding the fate of Sarovo Jews is in the early 1940s some 90 years later. It is likely that the reporter meant "the descendants" of those persons and others who were still living there that were murdered.

Page 80 and Page 117
[4] On July 26, 2009, a stone tablet dedicated to the Holocaust in Kamenets was unveiled and consecrated at the intersection of Chkalov and Prolytarskya Streets in Kamenets. The text in Belarusian reads, "To the everlasting memory of the victims of the Holocaust" and "In memory of the Jews - prisoners of the Nazi ghetto in the town of Kamenets in 1941 - 1942."

The translation of the tablet itself that is written in Hebrew reads:
In memory of the people slaughtered by the Nazis
Jews who lived in the Kamenets Ghetto
During the years of 1941-1942
May their souls be bound up in the bond of our lives

At the base of a stone there is an inscription in English:
This monument was erected through the efforts of Belarussian Jewish Community and thanks to the Simon Mark Lazarus Foundation, UK, the Miles and Marilyn Kletter Family Foundation, USA, the Warren and Beverly Geisler Family Foundation, USA.

Page 87

[5] See page 91 of the Yizkor Book of Kamenets. The Tragedy and Destruction of Kamenetz, a letter by Dora Galperin, gives a different version than does the author and identifies the person (P.) to be Fyodor Fanasevich in whose home Dora lived when, in 1940, the Communists threw the Galperin family out of their home. http://www.jewishgen.org/yizkor/kamenets/kam091.html

© G.S.Musevich
© Sherwin L. Sokolov, translation – 2014 - All Rights Reserved

www.ingramcontent.com/pod-product-compliance
Lightning Source LLC
Chambersburg PA
CBHW071707040426
42446CB00011B/1948